Heartache
and Healing

Coming to terms with grief

Heartache and Healing

Coming to terms with grief

Larry Yeagley

REVIEW AND HERALD® PUBLISHING ASSOCIATION
HAGERSTOWN, MD 21740

The author assumes full responsibility for the accuracy of all facts and quotations as
cited in this book.

This book was
Edited by Gerald Wheeler
Cover illustration and design by Bryan Gray
Typeset: 11/12.5 Times

PRINTED IN U.S.A.

99 98 97 96 95   10 9 8 7 6 5 4 3 2 1

R&H Cataloging Service
Yeagley, Lawrence Robert, 1933-
    Heartache and healing.

    1. Bereavement.   2. Grief.   I. Title.
            152.4

ISBN 0-8280-0881-7

Contents

Chapter One

Fading Footprints

A brisk wind pushed against me as I walked along Lake Michigan. Whitecaps on the gray-green water turned into spray. The angle of the sun made the dune grass stand out boldly against the light-brown sand. The whole scene was conducive to letting my thoughts roam at will.

A burning in my leg muscles signaled that I needed to retrace my steps. Facing the wind with head down at times, I noticed my footprints disappearing under the drifting sand. By the time I reached my starting point the wind had totally erased them.

I climbed halfway up the sand dune and leaned against a large black oak. Peering through its branches, I scanned the beach scene from a new perspective. Questions crowded my mind.

Are the days of my life like so many footprints? Does my life impact on other lives the way my feet made an impression on the sand? When I am gone, will time obscure my lifeprints? Will anyone remember me? Will there be some trace of me in other lives?

On his way to the seminary where he was in his fourth week of study in the Master of Divinity program, our son Jeff had been killed when a speeding 18-wheeler struck his car. A little boy attended our son's funeral. Later in the day the child asked his mother, "Will the Yeagleys forget Jeff?" I suspect the boy's real question was "Will you forget me if I die?"

Forgotten. What a lonely thought. Would you want to be forgotten? Can you bear the thought of being a faded footprint? Let me assure you that you will always live in the hearts of those who love you.

Fran called me four months after a freak accident crushed her son to death. "Larry, am I doing something wrong? I still have real strong pain, and I think about Andy a lot. Friends from church tell me I should not be thinking about him anymore. I've had some physical problems. When I went to my doctor, he said I probably need therapy. People give me the impression that I'm sick because I'm still thinking about Andy. What am I doing wrong?"

I told her she'd think about her son the rest of her life. Not to think about him would be to forget herself, because he is a very real part of her.

Our son died a little more than a decade ago, but I think of him every day. The emotional tone of those thoughts is much different than during the first two years without him, but his lifeprints show up in unexpected places.

Two years ago I was driving across the bridge in Charleston, South Carolina, to visit some World War II battleships berthed there. Suddenly tears welled up in my eyes as I told my wife how much Jeff would have enjoyed the ships. But by the time we arrived at the naval museum the tears were gone, and we enjoyed the day.

Our three other sons and their families visit us. We have satisfying fellowship that includes both fun and serious discussion, and I could not wish for a more rewarding experience. Yet after they leave I still find myself longing for a car to pull into the driveway. Not the same three cars that have already come and gone. The arrival of Jeff's car would make the fellowship complete. Hearing him chuckle and tell of his adventures would bring contentment. I'd feel secure, as I did when all four boys were tucked safely in their boyhood beds. Frequently I visualize his coming home. It's sad yet meaningful, because his footprints have not faded.

Chapter Two

Never the Same

Imet Lester in an old New England town. He had invited me
to accept a pastoral position in the three-state district over
which he presided. We visited the church and the parsonage. After a
brief interview with the chair of the search committee, we drove for
three hours to the local church headquarters. Lester's artful questions
and comments drew me out until he felt convinced of my compe-
tency for the job. At the same time I carefully sized him up and became convinced that I could work for him.

Twenty years later Lester held a very important administrative position. By now I lived more than 1,000 miles from that historic New
England town from which I had received his call. Now he asked me
to conduct a seminar for church leaders and their office assistants.

The first morning of the seminar Lester met me with his usual
warm smile and gracious greeting. It astonished me how little his
physical features had changed. I almost expressed my sentiments in
words, but then sensed a slight hint of difference about him.

That day we ate lunch at a quiet restaurant. Away from interrup-
tion, Lester admitted to taking me to lunch for selfish reasons. He
wanted me to listen to his heartache over the loss of his son. The accident had occurred years ago, but the death had left Lester a different person. The ugly scars had burned deep into his soul. "Will I ever
be the same?" he questioned.

The following two years I repeated that seminar. Each time I
shared a quiet lunch with Lester and learned to know his heart.

He was not the same man who met me in that New England town
for the first time. The harsh winds of life had carved awesome

canyons in his character, canyons made of a strange mixture of pain and gentleness. He would never be the same any more than the Grand Canyon would become the salt flats of Utah.

A new friend chatted with me six months after his wife died. "I think of her every minute of every day," he quietly confessed.

"I can understand that," I replied. "My son died more than 10 years ago, and I still think of him every day. Some days the thoughts are pleasant, and sometimes they are deeply sad."

"It's all right to think of her, isn't it?" he asked.

"As long as love is eternal, it is all right to think of a loved one," I replied.

Even when words are not spoken, the eyes and the facial features tell the story of loss. A person's sensitivity to the pain of others can also be the product of a biography of his or her own heartache.

Five years after Jeff died I was lecturing in California. A minister met me at lunch with a comment I didn't expect. "I heard you lecture before your son died. As I listened to you this morning I noticed a striking difference. I sensed a depth and a credibility that were missing before."

As I flew home from that seminar I struggled with his observation. I wanted to deny any change, but now I must admit a difference.

Fresh out of school, I had God figured out quite well. When I visited the sick, words flowed easily. Ideas picked up from my devotional reading poised on the tip of my tongue. Catchy phrases and tired clichés filled my ministerial vocabulary. Defending God was my major task when I visited a person broken by the realities of life.

Today I admit the shallowness of my knowledge. My earlier concepts of God now seem so elementary and inadequate. The questions of a broken heart remind me that I am a fellow questioner, not an answer man. I too am broken, not a flashy Christian who has it all together.

Now I understand why a young pastor came to only one session of a support group. Morris's two children had been in an accident. The daughter died instantly. An ambulance rushed the son to the hospital. Forty days in a row Morris placed his hands on his son and prayed for healing. On the forty-first day his son died. Unable to pray or preach, he took a leave of absence and did manual labor for a living. He came to the group and faced a barrage of answers before he could complete the questions.

After Jeff died, Morris read the obituary in the newspaper. He waited a few months, then stopped by my office. Five minutes into the conversation he said, "I'm sure you can help me now. The death of your son has changed you. I can trust you with my doubts and disbelief."

Until my own losses began to mount, the big question Why? prompted me to give people answers. Looking back on those days, I can remember the puzzled looks on the questioners' faces after I gave my easy answers. The Why? questions are now mine, and there are no adequate explanations. I no longer give easy answers.

I was colecturing with a seminary professor at an American Cancer Society conference. His wife had died six months before the conference. And his comments revealed that his loss had changed him too.

"I used to try to answer the Why? questions until my wife died. Now I know there are no adequate answers in the Bible to those questions. The Bible was written to show us how to get out of the mess we're in. I've found better questions for which I find answers in the Bible. Does God take my suffering seriously? If so, what has He done about it? What is He doing about it? What will He do about it? I am finding answers to those questions, and the answers bring me peace."

My Pennsylvania Dutch heritage conditioned me to keep my feelings to myself. My family exhibited few physical manifestations of affection.

During World War II my brother served in the Coast Guard. He'd come home on leave occasionally. When the time to return arrived, my parents, my brother, his girlfriend, and I rode in an old 1937 Pontiac to the train station in Lancaster. While waiting for the steam locomotive to pull in, we stood on the platform making small talk. Our voices never had a hint of emotion, nor did we have any physical contact.

When the smoky train hissed to a stop, we continued the small talk until the conductor yelled the final boarding call. A flurry of quick hugs and a few goodbyes, and my brother was off to New York. We shed a few guarded tears as we returned to the Pontiac; then life went on as usual.

The last time I saw Jeff was at the seminary where he had begun his graduate studies. I gave a lecture to a group of high school students, and he slipped into the hall to listen. Afterward, as we walked to my car, he told me about his orientation session coming up in an hour, and I chatted about my job. There was no physical contact, not even a hand on the shoulder. Then I drove away, looking out the side window momentarily to see him disappear.

Thousands of times in the past decade I have longed to have one more chance at that last visit. I would ask him if he was apprehensive about the orientation and then listen to his response. I would give him encouragement and affirm him for his accomplishments. Above all, I'd give him a hug before I climbed into my car.

Since his death I have attempted to overcome the stoicism of my heritage. By God's grace I am learning to share feelings verbally and physically. It isn't a change that comes easily, but I'm determined to do so.

Once I visited the Alabama-Coushatta Indian Reservation in the Big Thicket of east Texas. An elderly Indian took me for a ride through the dense woodland, stopping occasionally to familiarize me with a plant or a bird. Stopping the open-sided truck and turning off the engine, he quietly told me about an old friend he grew up with. They had many long conversations and played games together. When his heart ached, his friend always listened without passing judgment. Now his friend was gone, making the Big Thicket a lonely place. His voice trailed off into silence as he looked up toward the top of a giant loblolly pine. My eyes followed his gaze to behold the lifeless tree.

One fallen tree creates a gaping hole in a forest, making the woodland different, never to be the same again. A missing loved one changes the entire family system permanently, leaving each individual altered in some manner.

Scores of people in all age groups have told me they are not the same after some loss. Their lives are richer because of the way they responded to the heartache. All of them wish the positive changes had come down a different avenue. Even though they rejoice at the growth, they tell of an emptiness that isn't totally filled. They will never be the same.

Katrina decided to rebel against the change a loss always mandates. After a drunk driver killed her son, she told me, "I will be grieving for the rest of my life exactly as I am today. Nothing will heal my poor sick heart. How can I heal when my son is robbed of life, robbed by a drunk? I'll be miserable the rest of my life in spite of all the things you say about recovery."

She was miserable for the three years I remained in touch with her. A move on my part terminated my contact with her, but I have an idea she is still miserable. So are the people who live close to her. Her husband and daughter moved out of the house to escape her wrath.

When Ron and Faye lost their son, they determined to make the best of it and eventually to be helpful to couples with similar loss. They allowed grief to happen however it occurred. Lots of weeping and talking out feelings in their early grief began the readjustment quickly. Even during their time of most acute grief they took opportunities to reach out to others. Taking the focus off of self, it gave them a renewed sense of purpose and mission.

Many such changes are subtle and beyond our control, but we ourselves determine, in many cases, whether they are negative or positive. I've found much truth in the advice given to me by a chaplain supervisor. "Your loss is not the most important consideration—it's what you do with what's left."

Chapter Three

Saying Goodbye —A Long Process

Marcella had a difficult pregnancy. She knew it would be her only child, so volumes of dreams for the expected child accumulated during the nine months. She had the nursery furnishings finished for the big day and waited nervously. But then strange feelings came over her as she rode to the maternity hospital. The obstetrician confirmed those feelings when he told her the baby was in some trouble. Less than a day after the birth, Marcella found herself planning a funeral.

She knew only one way to handle the death. Moving far away, she tried to build a busy life for herself and get too involved in her exciting career to think. Thirty-five years later she couldn't escape the reality and was falling apart.

A friend gave her a copy of my book *Grief Recovery*. She read it eagerly until she came to the chapter entitled "Saying Goodbye," then threw the book into the corner of her bedroom and vowed never to pick it up again. She would not have her baby dead.

Her emotional state continued to deteriorate. A friend suggested going to the baby's grave. Marcella called her travel agent and discovered the long trip would be too costly. That night she looked at the book in the corner. *It would be a lot cheaper to read that chapter even though it's going to be very painful,* she thought.

After reading it over several times, she finally said aloud to herself, "This is what I should have started doing 35 years ago. I'm going to do it right now even if it does hurt like mad."

"I began to have a peace inside me that I had not had for many years," she told later. "If only someone had told me to say goodbye sooner!"

Saying goodbye to dreams that could never come true was the key to the grief locked inside her. The more she said goodbye to what could not be, the more mellow became the pain.

Even if Marcella had begun the farewells shortly after her baby's death, she would still have encountered periodic times of saying goodbye in the intervening years. Saying goodbye would have been helpful in handling her acute grief, but still more farewells faced her after I met her. This is to be expected.

Jeff spent 15 months doing a ministerial internship in New York. In spite of a very helpful mentor, he called me and discussed pastoral problems. When I visited him in New York, we looked at his pastoral options and discussed theological issues.

We went by to see a church member in the local veterans' hospital. The male nurse told Jeff that Al was in a coma and would not respond in any manner. But my son walked up to the bed and said in his usual happy voice, "Hi, Al, this is Jeff."

"Well, hello," came the prompt response. The two of them chatted the way they always did over Sunday morning breakfast. The amazed nurse was speechless.

Our two youngest sons are pastors. We spend time enjoying shop talk on the phone, go book shopping together, and manage to analyze parish problems during most visits.

This has prompted many farewells over the last few years. My dreams of watching the pastoral development of my oldest son will never be fulfilled. Those 15 months in New York were his only chance to explore the work he had chosen.

Ten years after his death I participated in the ordination of a young pastor. As the large group of ordained ministers circled around the young man, laid their hands on him, and prayed, a strange feeling came over me. Thoughts of Jeff's ordination that would never be filled my mind. Another farewell confronted me.

Graduations, weddings, births, family reunions, holidays, vacation trips, and scores of other special times hold moments of saying goodbye to what cannot be.

Dr. William Worden, author and researcher, presented a seminar in Muskegon, Michigan, in 1991. He described the process of saying goodbye as finding a place to put that important person, a place where he or she will always be remembered without interfering with the functions of life. He felt this was a gentler way of stating that we need to withdraw the emotional energy we invested in a relationship.

Frankly, I have no problem using the phrase "saying goodbye," because that's exactly what we need to do.

A chief of psychiatry invited me to speak to his residents in training. When I suggested the need to say goodbye to what can no longer be, one resident objected noisily.

After the young doctor quieted down, the chief spoke up in my defense. "You obviously haven't done your homework. Several books based on good research show that life is a series of hellos and goodbyes. Good emotional health equips us to do this. People who never say goodbye are the ones we need to be concerned about."

Goodbyes are healthy. They need to be sprinkled throughout the years of this life and actually increase the significance of the hellos.

Velita learned to say goodbye quickly and plans to experience a hello that will never be punctuated by another goodbye.

I met her in the maternity ward. The head of the bed was elevated, and she was carefully searching for something in her little black daybook. "What are you looking for?" I asked.

"I'm trying to find what I did to make my baby deformed. I've been looking for two days."

"Have you found anything?"

"No. The doctor said it wasn't anything I did, but I still wonder about it. I even searched my heart for sins against God. Maybe this is my punishment. But I know God wouldn't do that to a little baby."

"I understand you haven't allowed them to bring your baby to the room," I commented.

"That's right. I don't understand it, but I can't do it now," she said with a questioning tone.

"When you were a little girl, did you ever think about having a baby of your own?"

"Oh, yes. I was about 8."

"What did your baby look like?"

"She was long and pretty with dark hair and long eyelashes. Her eyes were dark brown. A real dream baby."

"In your teens you began dating. Was a baby part of your dreams?"

"Of course," she quickly replied with a little smile on her face.

"What did that baby look like?"

"Just the same. Yes, just the same."

"A few years ago you married. Did you dream of a baby?"

"On our honeymoon. I saw her in my mind. The same baby."

"The baby in the nursery—do you see her in your mind?"

"Yes, I do. She's the same baby I dreamed of having when I was a girl."

"Velita, is it possible that you need to say goodbye to the baby of your dreams before you can say hello to the baby you received two days ago?"

I waited while Velita wept. Her body shook with pain and disappointment. Eventually she squeezed out a few words. "You're right, but I don't know how to say goodbye."

"I'll teach you how," I promised.

During the next half hour Velita rehearsed all her dreams for her baby. Addressing the imagined infant, she bid a tearful farewell to what could never be: a perfectly healthy first baby.

Within a day she welcomed her own real child. Bonding began at once. The nursing staff gave both of them a special send-off.

Months later I was called early in the morning to Velita's tiny house. She sat on the couch wrapping her infant in one blanket after another. Her husband stood in the doorway, frozen with shock. The funeral director waited in a corner, holding a little basket lined with a pink quilt.

"Why all the blankets, Velita?" I asked.

"I don't want her to get cold. She's still warm. I won't let her get cold. The man said he'll keep her warm."

I squeezed her arm gently and sat quietly while she wept softly. In a little while she lifted her head and looked at me intently.

"In the hospital you told me I needed to say goodbye to the baby of my dreams so I could say hello to the baby I received. That's what I did. Now I need to say goodbye to the baby I received so I can say hello to the perfect baby of my dreams when I go to heaven."

Quietly she whispered to the tiny infant wrapped in several blankets. She asked me to pray. When I finished, she handed the little body to the funeral director. He tucked it into the basket with the touch of a mother. Before he carried her out to the car he said, "We'll be very careful with her."

Velita watched out the window until the car disappeared. Slowly she turned toward the bedroom and fell into the arms of her husband. Saying goodbye and hello had taken its toll, but as I drove home I was encouraged by Velita's hope of a permanent hello.

Over the past decade I have said goodbye to many strands of my relationship with Jeff. The energy required is beyond measuring, but the process has freed emotional energy to invest in other young men in ministry.

As other strands of the relationship will come to my attention in the future, I will say more goodbyes and enrich my life with still more hellos. Like Velita, I look forward to a permanent hello with Jeff.

Chapter Four

Loneliness

A powerful longing for home suddenly shadowed over me like a thundercloud. I yearned to jump into my car and drive there, but I couldn't decide where or what home was.

Could it be the old Cornwall farmhouse with the wainscot around the kitchen wall and the coal-burning cookstove to one side? Or was it picking the strawberries beside the railroad tracks and cherries from trees along the fence rows?

Maybe home was the 18-room plantation house along the Susquehanna River. Taking a long ride in my coaster wagon from the top of the orchard hill to the barnyard might satisfy me. But we lived there only one year. I could scarcely call it home.

The Jonestown farm, of course. The red Farmall F-14. The trails through the meadow and pine forest. The swims in Swatara Creek. Learning to drive in Daddy's 1941 Studebaker. Sitting in a one-room schoolhouse and learning eighth-grade math from squinty-eyed Mr. Fake. Was this the home I longed for?

Suddenly the thought came to me. Home is not a place. Home is an intricate weaving of relationships held together by two special people I call Mom and Daddy. But the warp and woof of that fabric have become undone. Their deaths have pulled out the dominant threads in the cloth. The home I long for exists only in my mind. Roads cannot take me back.

I cannot live in that home of the past, I told myself. Instead I am one of the principal threads in the fabric my children and grandchildren call home. Unless I live and love creatively in the present, home will not exist for them.

My little 3-year-old granddaughter ran into my arms. We hugged tight, and I told her, "Jamie, you are my special friend."

She squeezed me very tight and said, "Yeah, Grandpa, and we'll be faithful."

That's when I realized that I am part of home. My existence, as it brings beauty into another person's life, is home. Not a town or a farmhouse in rural Pennsylvania. I carry home within me. It consists of many qualities felt by those I love. As I generously give to those around me, home becomes a living reality.

Home is not static. It forever changes as I change and accept the changes in others. My perception of home can either create loneliness or instill a deep sense of purpose.

But such an insight on loneliness was slow in developing. Between my present philosophy and the death of my parents loneliness occurred countless times when it cast its shadow over me. Not a despairing loneliness, but an indescribable sense of incompleteness. Being deprived of my parents' presence made its mark. They occupied space within me that others will never fill. In time, I reconciled myself to that fact.

Sometimes a more pronounced loneliness strikes us like a left uppercut from a boxer. A person we lived with for years or hoped to live with for years dies, divorces us, or moves away. This painful loss of close relationship drastically transforms our usual life patterns. Suddenly we become aware of needs that relationship had met that we were previously unaware of or that we took for granted. A painful emptiness acutely strikes us in the gut.

Such loneliness results from being deprived of intimacy and community. Some people tell me they were not conscious of the loneliness during the first few weeks of their loss because they were numb. But two or three months afterward it finally strikes them. And for a long time after the loss new implications of it continually manifest themselves, thus perpetuating the loneliness.

Grieving people need to be very realistic and accept the idea that loneliness will be with them for a long time. This doesn't indicate weakness, but that love has truly formed a bond. When that bond breaks, we must expect tremors and aftershocks. A commitment to love a person includes a commitment to experience loneliness when the bond severs.

During the long months and years after a loss, advice to the lonely comes so glibly. "You just need to keep busy." "Get out and meet people." "Volunteer!" "Get a good hobby." All the free advice seems to imply a personal defect in the lonely person.

I fell into conversation with an English woman as we waited for our flights out of Detroit. She had spent the past 10 years in Detroit, but on her sixtieth birthday she decided to return to her native country.

"Why England after 10 years in the U.S.A.?" I asked.

"You want me to die a lonely old woman? You Americans produce loneliness. You isolate old people in nursing homes, housing for the elderly, and suburbs removed from people centers. Public transportation is very limited, virtually locking old people in cells. Forget that. I'm returning to London, where I can walk to market every morning to buy a bit of food and pass the news with neighbors."

"Are you telling me that loneliness is a societal problem in America?"

"Indeed!" she quipped. "You make it very easy to die in loneliness."

My English friend was right. Modern society does greatly exacerbate loneliness, especially after the loss of a relationship. Since most of us don't have the option of moving to a more ideal area, we must face loneliness with a determination to rise above it.

Talking about loneliness is counterproductive. Rehearsing your loneliness to others only sinks you deeper into despair and drives friends away.

Arlene spent the first two years after her husband's death whining about her loneliness. During the course of an evening she would tell several of her friends her woeful story and spiral herself as deep as she could plummet into despair. Finally I challenged her to make a decision to build a new community to replace the married couples who had dropped out of sight. She accepted the challenge.

On her way out of the food market she saw a handsome young man carrying a sign—"Will work for food." On impulse she took him home and put him to work in her flower garden.

Over a big bowl of soup and man-sized sandwiches Arlene found her way into the young man's heart. His father had died a year earlier, sending him on an aimless journey. But Arlene saw potential in her new friend. Within a year he became like a son. Their friendship became a permanent relationship.

She enrolled in a local university, but soon discovered how unsuited she was for such a fast pace. While attending classes she met young women who needed mothering. Her empty bedrooms were soon occupied, and her kitchen became a center for pizza parties.

Arlene's decision to build community provided many types of intimacy for her. She was both its giver and receiver. Wholeness returned to her. Her capacity to live and love creatively expanded, which in turn gave her a sense of purpose.

Soon she found herself in relationships in which she was no longer a pitiful leaner but standing tall and allowing people to enjoy her companionship.

Arlene's story is not to suggest that loneliness never again came knocking at her door. She had moments when she entered the doldrums, but she had set her course. A decision to take charge of loneliness instead of allowing it to take charge of her was her lifesaver.

During the four years after her husband died, Arlene developed into the person she dreamed of becoming. Her deep state of maturity ultimately carried over into the relationship that culminated in her remarriage.

Unrealistic expectations can throw saddened people into a loneliness loop. My family and I experienced that loop when we moved to Texas.

Two years after our son died I took a position in a Texas hospital. The small community we lived in consisted of professional and retired people. Most of them were members of the large church I attended.

We had high expectations of many friends, but the only warm friendship demonstrated to us came from the official greeter at the church door. People seemed to know each other, but we attended for six weeks without the slightest bit of recognition from anyone else. Loneliness set in, and we cursed the church over our lunch every Sabbath.

After six weeks of coldness in the July-hot Texas town, a woman turned to thank me for holding the door for her one day. "Thank you! You folk must be new here. We'll have to get together socially."

Although I don't remember what I said to her, I was surprised and hopeful. We never socialized with her, but it broke the silence. That little exchange at the door started some thinking on my part.

I realized that busy professionals need time alone on the weekend. They weren't ignoring me, but simply trying to survive their hectic schedules. My expectations relaxed, and the loneliness eased.

Loneliness is the tagalong problem of grief. For years I've studied grieving people to determine what inherent characteristics of grief might possibly perpetuate and exacerbate loneliness.

Here are some of the leading culprits:

1. The tendency to withdraw from people.
2. Inability to experience pleasure—indeed, a deliberate avoidance of it.
3. Self-pity.
4. Dumping on people before developing a trust level and agreeing on ground rules for the sharing of painful feelings.
5. Showering innocent people with our displaced anger.
6. Failure to set new goals.
7. Inadequate social and communication skills.
8. A misunderstanding of solitude.
9. A narrow perception of intimacy.
10. A lack of balanced dialogue.

A few of these points are not strictly grief behaviors, however. They are preexisting situations compounded by the experience of loss. A brief elaboration of each of these areas will be helpful.

The tendency to withdraw from people removes you from others just when you need them desperately. A certain amount of withdrawal is helpful during acute grief because it conserves energy and provides time for private mourning. But getting into the recluse syndrome can develop during acute grief and carry over into the months and years of residual grief.

A Texan took care of this by making an agreement with a few friends. They promised to "give him the point of their cowboy boots if he ever took to the lounge chair for too long." Rustling him up in the morning, together they caught up on the news down at the coffee shop.

Inability to experience pleasure is a component of depression. Since grief is a reactive depression—one caused by something else—it's logical that your ability to find anything humorous would plummet to a low ebb.

Giving yourself permission to laugh is essential. If you can't find pleasure yet, however, don't panic. But always permit yourself to have it when it does eventually. Then when you do experience it you won't be as alarmed or guilt-ridden.

Whatever you do, don't spend months reading dozens of books on grief. Instead read a variety of good books, including ones on humorous topics.

Listening to Garrison Keillor's monologues about his mythical Lake Wobegon restored my pleasure potential. Laughter with other people lowers our guard, and we come closer together. Surprisingly, laughter can be a funny way of crying for some of us.

Self-pity is allowable in acute grief, but continuing it beyond six months will evaporate the friendships you need to prevent loneliness.

Tressa stopped by my office frequently during her first two years of widowhood. Her entire conversation expressed self-pity uttered with an annoying whine. I was rapidly growing weary of her recitation of friends departed.

"Tressa, have you ever listened to your voice on a tape recording?"

"Why?" she whined.

"I think you should. You speak with an irritating whine. I have a hunch you are driving people away with your self-pity and your whining."

Tressa cut her visit short and didn't return for months. One day she stopped to eat at the hospital cafeteria and introduced me to her new boyfriend—in a pleasing voice.

For two years after Jeff died I served as a chaplain in a psychiatric hospital. Seven years after that I worked in a general hospital with an active emergency room. Believe me, I experienced my share of self-pity, but focusing on the tragic problems of others helped to put my own in perspective. I actually felt needed and valuable to others, which alleviated much of the loneliness.

Dumping on people before developing a trust level is a sure way of driving them away. I've run from quite a few people who share all of their tragedies in the first hour of our first meeting. Such premature disclosure is downright frightening. It's nice to have a few ground rules that provide you with some control over your time and privacy. Trust levels and ground rules for sharing will deepen relationships and prevent loneliness.

Showering people with our displaced anger destroys most relationships. Very rarely does a friend see the grief behind the anger and stay by. Usually the recipient won't stick around for a second blow. The result is lost relationships and loneliness.

Failure to set new goals leaves us without purpose in life. Awakening each morning then becomes pointless. We will have no contact with people of common interests simply because we have put life on hold.

After our son died I felt like putting life on hold permanently. I felt dead inside. While I was in this state a seminary professor called me. "Larry, I'm swamped with my teaching load. Could you possibly take a class for me next quarter?"

Somewhat reluctantly I agreed. During the next three months I studied and developed a curriculum outline. My study brought healing to me. A sense of usefulness and purpose returned. As I imagined a large class in front of me while I carefully prepared each lecture, my excitement grew.

On the first day of class my late son's classmates gathered in the large room where Jeff had excitedly launched his graduate program. I was determined to give them tools that could enlarge their skills. They must make up for their lost classmate who would not bless the world with his compassion and love. Determination to develop their excellence in ministry became almost a passion for me.

My students were my friends. As they shared themselves with me and I with them, the loneliness in my heart subsided. Some of them invited me to their tiny apartments for a meal. One student and his wife presented me with a pot full of marigolds. The students rose to their feet during the last class to thank me for sharing myself with them. I was surrounded by an unforgettable class of young men who took away the sting of my loneliness. To this day I am thankful for my professor friend's offer of a new goal.

My neighbors stopped by one day to chat about the death of their adult child. For three years they had taken her to dozens of therapists. Hopes climbed and plunged many times. Always there lingered the possibility of a cure.

"How is her death touching the relationship between the two of you?" I asked.

"We're getting along real well," the wife offered. "It's just that a terrible loneliness overpowers me—not because of anything he's doing or not doing."

The husband looked into the wife's teary eyes, then glanced at me with a look of lostness in his face.

"We spent long hours with her and were really working hard to get her well," he said. "Now there is nothing to do, nothing to work for."

"We want to find something we can do to help other young women," the wife said. "We need a cause. I don't know what it can be yet, but for months I've sensed that we must do something in our girl's honor and memory."

They had discovered that setting new goals is a healing pathway.

Inadequate social and communication skills can contribute to loneliness for all of us, especially if a serious loss has stunned us.

If you find this your problem, I recommend attending a support group that encourages verbal sharing. There you'll meet other people with the same limitations. With the help of an experienced facilitator, you can learn the necessary skills and practice them in a safe environment.

A young woman who lost her father attended a group I conducted. The third week she told us that her husband noticed a great change in her. She never shared anything with anyone, but once she took the risk of disclosing her painful feelings to the groups, she wasn't nearly as tense. Soon she discovered she could say what she felt. People with similar feelings reached out to her, and she noticed that loneliness didn't have the death grip it had had on her before.

A misunderstanding of solitude leads us to run away from an experience essential to self-acceptance and personal development. Both hinge heavily on relationship building, which we must have to combat loneliness.

During early grief many people hate to be alone. If they must be by themselves, they play the stereo or TV to fill the silence. Henri J. M. Nouwen observed that many Americans are afraid of the "noise of silence." Yet befriending solitude holds some of the keys to living with loss.

A year after Jeff died I longed for time alone. A voice deep within called me to the quaint town of Shipshewana, Indiana. There I spent the early morning listening to the din of six auctioneers selling thousands of used household items. The antique Singer sewing machines, butter churns, canning jars, and furniture reminded me of my boyhood, when life was much simpler. Conversing with dozens of Amish farmers transported me mentally to the happy days in Cornwall, Pennsylvania.

My morning of reminiscing I punctuated with lunch at a quiet Pennsylvania German restaurant. Oatmeal pecan pie lingered on my taste buds as I slowly drove into the Indiana countryside.

I chanced upon a homemade sign—"Apples." An arrow pointed down a dirt road. After three miles of dust clouds spewing up from the rear of my Ford, I arrived at a weather-beaten house and barn. Attached to the barn was a map of the orchard designating the Spy, Winesap, and Cortland sections. The bottom of the sign listed the price and invited customers to drop the money in a slot by the kitchen door.

Not another soul was in the orchard. The brisk wind turned the October-dry cornfield next to the orchard into a veritable concert hall. At the top of a three-legged ladder I found myself surrounded by Winesaps and solitude. The picking took hours because I had no containers. Tying knots in the arms of my jacket and zipping it up created a makeshift bucket. Countless trips from tree to car trunk never registered on my mind. My thoughts were engaged in the stuff of life.

Surrounded by apples, I could picture Jeff high up in an apple tree in Climax, Michigan. It was two summers before his death. He was reciting his lines in a college drama. "Where is Godot?" he yelled at the top of his voice. I tried to imagine hearing his voice on the wind in the solitude of the orchard, but I would not hear his voice again. Atop that wobbly ladder I accepted that reality in my heart. The wind swept the tears across my cheeks, but with my heart I knew he was gone.

Two days after his death I had loudly scolded God for His lack of power to stop the speeding truck, but in that Indiana orchard I sensed an increasing reconciliation with God. My questions loomed like storm clouds, but the music of the cornfield and the ever-changing clouds against autumn-blue sky assured me that God has a design in life even if we are unable to see it. In time I would understand.

Alone through the windswept grass of the orchard I walked and talked aloud to the God who was present at last. I was not forsaken.

Driving home on a nearly-empty highway, I watched the setting sun turn the western sky into deep shades of pink and orange. Life seemed a little more together and at peace.

Nouwen pictures the inestimable value of creative solitude in these words:

"Somewhere we know that without a lonely place our lives are in danger. Somewhere we know that without silence words lose their meaning, that without listening speaking no longer heals, that without distance closeness cannot cure" (*Out of Solitude* [Notre Dame, Ind.: Ave Maria Press, 1974], p. 15).

A narrow perception of intimacy leaves us lonely even while surrounded by family.

The sexual revolution and the crass boldness of Hollywood clearly picture intimacy as the union of sexual organs. Despite such claims many people are dying of loneliness and are starved for intimacy while experiencing coitus daily. There has to be more.

Guy Greenfield gets to the heart of intimacy when he says, "Emotional intimacy might be described not as the touching of the hands but the touching of the hearts of each other" (*We Need Each Other* [Grand Rapids: Baker Book House, 1984], p. 154).

I was delighted with Greenfield's "dimensions of intimacy" because I had been asking my support groups to expand their understanding of intimacy. Many participants found this to be a way out of loneliness.

My friend Steve and I enjoy *intellectual intimacy*. We have shared challenging books and new theories of pastoral care for years. Quite a few volumes in my library are well read and marked as a result of our friendship.

Aesthetic intimacy would aptly describe the fire that burns in the hearts of me and my son David. During my somewhat lonely sojourn in Texas we livened up the concert hall of Fort Worth Symphony Orchestra. After what David's cello teacher called "a real barn burner," we shouted "Bravo," shaming the graying concertgoers into applause by our spontaneous eruptions. We talked about some concerts for months. Most of them have been the topics of our conversations for years.

Creative intimacy comes by building something together. The play of kids at the beach teaches us about this. A sand castle seen at first only in their dreams now takes shape under their hands. While they mold their castle, their kid hearts are open to sharing all sorts of deep matters. I know. I helped two little girls create such a structure. The Lake Michigan waves crumbled the castle, but their intimacy thrived. My life was blessed as well.

Waterslides, steam train trips, excursions to historic villages, badminton games, and backpacking are just a few of the recreational pursuits that have been a source of intimacy for our family. *Recreational intimacy,* Greenfield calls it.

In conversations with lonely people I often ask them if they take time to play. Most of them have forgotten how to do it. They have buried the little child deep inside.

When we are lonely we must force ourselves to play. I've heard it said that it's easier to act your way into a new way of feeling than it is to feel your way into a new way of acting.

One of my favorite activities as a hospital chaplain was playing with lonely hospitalized children. We made paper airplanes and turned their rooms and halls into airports. That was good medicine.

My boys and I climbed Sleeping Giant Mountain. From a distance the New England-sized mountain looked like a man in a prone position. We pretended we were sitting on the giant's ears and forehead. I sensed a special closeness to my little boys as we trudged up the mountain.

Work intimacy is a togetherness that results from sharing a job, a project, or a special venture. Loneliness never bothered me when I worked with my father on the farm. Harvesting our grain with our combine was a job that welded a bond between us. Daddy drove the tractor, and I sat on the combine tying the full bags of grain. Noise from the machinery kept us from speaking, but occasionally Daddy would give me a big grin when I dumped the full bags at the right spot. A pheasant flew up once in a while. That brought pointing motions and laughter from both of us. At the end of the day we sat down to supper like two equals, even though he had many years on me.

Crisis intimacy may sound strange, but those who have lost a loved one know it well. People facing conflict or crucial decisions together develop strong ties. Farmers in my home state of Pennsylvania will come to the aid of a family who loses a barn by fire. The men spend several days rebuilding the barn. The women cook the "seven sweets and seven sours" and other mouthwatering dishes. As many as 10 families draw together and restore both barn and broken spirits.

Commitment intimacy is not limited to marriage. Two or more people devoted to a common cause feel a kinship that holds loneliness at bay.

Stunt kite flying breeds a commitment that is infectious. When I took my kite to Lake Michigan for its initial voyage the glare of the sun on the light sand made it impossible to see my lines. They were twisted, but I couldn't tell which way to turn the line holders to straighten them out. Another kite flyer came running to my rescue. In moments my pink-and-blue wonder was aloft, and my new friend and I chatted about his six kites.

Spiritual intimacy has come to have new meaning for me. My son and I both pastored two small churches in the same area. Forming a cooperative pastorate, we shared pulpits, presented joint workshops, and planned music festivals. We talked about theological questions and church policy, and at times explored issues that bordered on rank heresy. It beats the horrid task of caring for the saints with not another soul to bounce things around with. That can be a lonely job.

My idea of deep spiritual intimacy is two people who can encourage each another on the journey to the God's kingdom without demanding that the other wear the same kind of shoes. A person's relationship with God is extremely special and unique. That's as it should be. Each person enhances the other's spiritual pleasure.

Communication intimacy is a part of all types of intimacy, but it is vital enough to treat separately. It can be either verbal or nonverbal. The deeper the relationship, the more frequently nonverbal communication occurs.

Many of the people who attend my bereavement support groups tell me their desire for communication has changed because of the loss. Their tolerance for shallow chitchat has lessened.

Marty came to see me for three years after her husband died. She frequently told me, "I simply can't run to the bridge clubs I used to love. The conversations are superficial. Life is too short to fritter it away talking a bunch of nonsense."

A lack of balanced dialogue also compounds loneliness. The "communication of intimacy" is what Dr. James J. Lynch calls dialogue. He says dialogue is the "elixir of life." That means sharing all that life is and means to you with another person.

Dr. Paul Tournier referred to this as "transparency." Transparency puts feelings into words and doesn't make the other person guess about your emotions. Two people in dialogue see words as symbols of values, beliefs, hopes, dreams, and negative and positive emotions.

People who have lost something important in their lives find themselves forced to sift out the chaff in order to savor the precious grain of life. They need to find relationships in which this deeper sharing occurs.

Grief leaves people exhausted for many months. Having neither energy nor desire to restructure life, they continue living as usual which makes them sharply aware of the voids caused by their loss. Loneliness lingers as long as those voids predominate or go unfilled.

For this reason I encourage people to begin actively grieving as soon and as intensely as possible. Then I encourage them to reorganize life and set new goals. This brings them back into the mainstream of life and prevents them from slipping into reclusive behavior.

Lingering loneliness is bound to happen, but the lingering will be shorter if we take charge of reshaping life.

Chapter Five

Anger Revisited

Elaine walked into my support group wearing a heavy winter coat. She never removed it during the first session. Her body rigid, she sat on the edge of her chair most of the time, and her eye contact with me was minimal. When she spoke, her words were clipped and sharp, but she smiled all the time. Everything about her demeanor gave me the message "Confront me, and I'll walk out."

For five weeks she listened intently, then slowly her defenses dropped and the tears began to flow. She began to drape her coat over the back of her chair. Finally she surrendered her determination to be in control of all things at all times.

"My son's death is the reason I came to this program," she shared. "I know he's gone. I can't change that. I believe I have made a good adjustment to that. But losing my son makes me think I may be angry at my mother. Does that sound terrible to you?"

"What leads you to suspect anger as a problem?" I asked.

"Well, my mother was never a mother to me. As long as I can remember, I took care of my younger siblings. She ignored anything serious that happened in our home. Although I was upset most of my growing-up years, I still never wanted to believe that I was angry at her! You don't get angry at your mother! But since I've been facing my son's death, I've had a strong sense of anger toward her."

For Elaine, losing a son triggered fresh grief reactions of anger about her loss of a mother-daughter relationship. That loss had begun 50 years earlier, but the reactions were now powerful and painful. The sudden upsurge of grief surprised her, and it greatly relieved her to know that her belated anger was not unusual.

Over the following years Elaine and I talked openly about her experience. She concluded that she had often felt anger over the years, but she would not allow herself to think that maybe her mother would never give her what she wanted. So she dealt with the anger by telling herself that she needed to be a better daughter. Then her mother would be a real parent.

Eventually Elaine gave herself permission to blame her mother for negligence and irresponsibility as a parent. She and her mother discussed the relationship until the mother admitted her faults and Elaine decided to stop searching for a parental closeness that would likely never exist.

At a support group meeting Elaine shared her victory. "I decided to do something about my angry feelings toward my mother. We had a good talk, and I can't describe how free I am now. I feel in control. It's a light feeling—that's what it is. I've felt like a little girl for years. Why didn't I learn sooner? I guess some things take longer to learn than others."

However troubling it may be to experience periodic acute grief reactions many months or years after a loss, it is not uncommon, nor does it indicate that a person is not making satisfactory adjustment to the loss.

Researchers S. Zisook, M. Click, and R. DeVaul suggested in 1982 in *American Journal of Psychiatry* that grief and mourning often last longer than believed. In 1985 and 1986 S. R. Shucter joined with S. Zisook in reports to *General Hospital Psychiatry* and *Psychiatric Annals* on research that suggested that some symptoms of mourning continue many years after a death.

It pleased me to learn of this research because it confirmed what I have myself observed in support groups and in the hospitals in which I worked. For years I had noticed that grief and mourning reactions fluctuated in frequency and intensity over periods of many years, not just months.

This long-term fluctuation was especially noticeable in sudden, traumatic losses. Other, later types of loss would prompt new reactions or renew earlier ones. With adequate support and encouragement, however, my acquaintances would meet these temporary experiences constructively.

This prolongation of mourning really makes sense if you stop to think of it. Consider the man who married an 18-year-old beauty in 1915. They brought four children into the world and managed to educate them in spite of the Great Depression. Sons and grandsons went to war. Some returned, and some did not. Good times and bad times on an Iowa farm left them with moderate prosperity. Life together tilling the soil bonded them securely until her death after 55 years of marriage.

At 75, 55 years after their wedding, it's impossible to bring the thousands of memories, hopes, dreams, joys, and sorrows up for full review in a short one-year period. For years fresh memories and important family events will prompt new grief. The passing of time is bound to bring to mind values and meanings in that long relationship that memory could not retrieve in a shorter time.

Therese A. Rando refers to this mourning process as "subsequent temporary upsurges of grief" (STUG). She observes that it is a part of uncomplicated mourning and should not be mistaken for complicated mourning—*Treatment of Complicated Mourning* (Research Press, 1993). This view of mourning helps us to understand why hundreds of feelings keep coming up in the years following a loss.

People in mourning have often worried about recurring anger. They ask, "Why can't I shake this anger?" Some revisit or regain their anger through repeatedly going over and over the same aspect of the loss. In most cases, though, new aspects of the loss will just suddenly appear as time passes, and the anger then has a different cause.

A woman attended a support group after her husband committed suicide. She had experienced anger for years, but not in response to the same things. Her initial anger was at her husband for killing himself. Weeks after the funeral she became furious because he had refused to share financial matters with her. The bills were piling up, but she didn't know how to pay them. An accountant friend of her late husband then helped her put affairs in order and taught her how to manage day-to-day finances. But when she studied her husband's financial dealings, she discovered that he had made risky and questionable business dealings that now jeopardized her future security. Again she was angry.

Three months after the death she became very lonely. During her loneliest time of the day she read novels about people madly in love. That started thoughts of how her husband had sealed himself off from her for days at a time while he was making money. Then she felt angry because he had robbed her of intimacy. A year after the loss she rummaged through the garage and saw his fishing rods and golf clubs. Again the anger returned because he had never shared his hobbies with her. The anger thus reappeared for years, but it came through many doors.

Since anger is such a common reaction to loss and is experienced over a long time after the loss, we should carefully define it. Neil Clark Warren views anger as a physical state of readiness, preparation, and power—a response to something or someone who causes fear, threatens to destroy our equilibrium, or hurts us or frustrates what we view to be important to our well-being—*Make Anger Your Ally* (Walgemuth and Hyatt, Inc., 1990).

When we are angry, we are prepared to act with power. We are prepared to cope with the situation facing us.

Early scholars of anger taught that we are at its mercy. They claimed that anger and aggression are inseparable and instinctual and regarded anger aggression as an inherited drive. Bottle it up, they reasoned, and you'll develop a slush fund for destructive lashing out later. Instead, vent it as it comes, they argued, and you will remain healthy.

If you read the works of Leonard Berkowitz, Albert Bandura, and Carol Tavris, however, you'll see a major shift from earlier definitions. Such authorities now recognize that we are different than the lower animals. We can choose the course of action we follow when a threatening event arouses anger. Decision-making is our special gift. As various aspects of loss arouse anger, we are not at its mercy. Instead we have hope of obtaining control of such anger expressions. We make the decisions that can bring personal growth rather than anger habits and bitter resentment.

The psychological sciences no longer consider the earlier ideas of catharsis as valid. Pounding pillows, chopping wood, fantasized aggression, and watching other people aggress (as on TV and boxing matches) do not drain away some kind of inner drive state. Instead, all aggression only begets more aggression. I saw a living demonstration of this when I spoke to a chapter of a nationwide support group for victimized people.

The leader of the group met me in the hotel lobby and escorted me to the meeting room. As he walked along, he informed me that, unlike all other people in loss, the people in his group were angry and would not appreciate it if I tried to take their anger away. "We have a right to be angry the rest of our lives," he added.

Despite his comment, I did not change my approach as I talked about the danger of rehearsing injuries over and over until anger becomes a vicious habit that turns into bitter resentment and hatred. This, I emphasized, was a sure way to become our own victimizer, inflicting long-term pain perhaps never even intended by the perpetrator of the crime.

The leader and his wife were furious. They went to the coffeepot, filled their cups, and were too angry to find their chairs again.

After the session ended, a young woman approached my son and asked if the speaker was his father. Then she said, "Tell your dad to keep the pressure on. The leaders of this group are my parents. I lived at home when my sister was murdered, and I felt all the pain. But eventually my parents' anger turned our home into a living hell. I recently moved out to avoid being a victim of their anger."

I have never apologized for telling people that pain is inevitable but that suffering is our choice. We decide what we will do with the grief reactions that present themselves to us over the span of our mourning.

According to James W. Pennebaker, obsessive dwelling on traumatic events and long-term rehearsal of injuries usually consist of poorly organized and incomplete reactions. Such thoughts may be vague, fragmented, and nightmarish (*Handbook of Life Stress* [New York: Wiley, 1988]).

Bereaved spouses who handled their losses in this manner had more health problems than those who confronted the feelings openly and thoroughly. When the spouses wrote down their thoughts or articulated them in conversation, the event took on structure and focus. The process of assimilating the loss, learning from it, and then going on with life was then much more likely to happen. The benefits of journaling and openly discussing periodic anger is not from catharsis, but from the insight gained from the exercise itself.

Many of the bereaved people I have known continued to struggle with anger because they had molded their lost loved one into a marble saint. Their restructuring of the relationship included only the ideal characteristics. It was what they wished it had always been, not what it actually was. "Are there any parts of the relationship that you'd classify as so-so, mildly unbearable, or downright upsetting?" I'd ask them.

"Oh no. Our marriage was a perpetual honeymoon. Really! I can't think of anything I disliked about him." I have listened to many of these claims in utter disbelief.

Months or years go by. One day the memory bumps into a negative episode, and anger is the natural response.

Many relationships are ambivalent. Thus feelings of anger are bound to occur both before and after the loss of the relationship. We must allow the marble saint to shatter if we are to confront the subsequent anger constructively.

Anger especially revisits those who experienced losses that were then followed by trails of litigation and drawn-out court proceedings. This produces an eternal flow of painful new information that keeps reopening old wounds and inflicting new ones. In most cases assimilating such realities and then moving on with life requires a strong support system, and in some cases ongoing professional guidance.

Loss is something we cannot prevent entirely. We cannot change that fact, but we can alter the way we view and react to loss. To this extent we must have some control so that we can keep our anger from becoming our master.

During the Second World War my grade-school companions were addicted to the game of marbles. Recesses always found clusters of children clutching leather marble pouches. Every bare spot in the lawn bore a circle engraved by stick or penknife. Each empty cement bike stall was graced with a chalk line and a circle.

I still remember my first pouch of "glassies." I had visions of walking home from school with my pouch bulging and my pockets weighted down as well. But alas, I went home only with an empty pouch stuffed into my pocket and an empty feeling in my stomach. Weeping with my mother and venting my anger, I vowed to hate those boys and girls who had carried my marbles home.

My mother asked one question. "Did you play for keeps?"

"Yes."

"If you play for keeps, you stand a chance of losing. If you can't learn to lose, you shouldn't play for keeps."

That was bitter medicine.

Since I was the school's poorest shot, I knew I'd never return home with a full pouch. I'd have to change my perspective.

A few days later I went to McCrory's five-and-ten-cent store and selected a mesh bag of the prettiest cat's-eyes I could find. In the morning I went to school with a full pouch.

The kids gathered around me and admired my glassies. I was popular. At recess I rationed my marbles, determined to quit playing when I reached my quota. One pouch of marbles lasted me two weeks. I lost marbles every day, but I had friends as well.

A short fat kid who lived on the road to our farm never played marbles and wasn't accepted by the other kids. He must have been hungry for friendship when he invited me to his house. From a cupboard he pulled a jar full of the prettiest glassies I'd ever seen. One after another he pulled his favorites out for me to see.

"I'll tell ya what," he said. "I'll give ya a dozen marbles and a shooter. I'll make a circle on the rug with this string and we'll play, but not for keeps. When we quit playing, you'll put all the marbles back into the jar."

In less than an hour I was bored and ready to go home. I preferred playing for keeps because I had learned to lose.

In the game of life nothing is for keeps, but learning to face loss has its gains. Changing perspectives can keep us in the game. It's better than dropping out.

Chapter Six

~

Changing Perspective

Edwin and June felt their life come to a screeching halt when their 19-year-old daughter died in a car crash. June was inconsolable, and Edwin tried to be a Gibraltar of stoic calm. But his wife's emotional roller-coaster ride began to erode his own fragile emotional base. So he decided to give her some diversionary activity on a special anniversary.

"Honey, I took the day off just for you," he said. "Now, you tell me something you'd really like to do, and we'll spend the whole day doing what makes you happy."

Immediately June broke into tears as she said, "I don't want to do anything. If our little girl were alive she'd be here to congratulate us. She's gone, and life is never going to be the same again."

As Edwin told me about this conversation, he and June were attending a support group. Putting his head on his knees, he said, "Here I took the whole day off, and the whole day was a big waste. Just a big waste."

"May I help you change your perspective?" I asked.

"Something needs to change," he responded. "After a whole day of crying and a whole lot of disappointment, I need something."

"You started your special anniversary with a fixed agenda, but June's all-day crying jag wasn't on your agenda. That's why you see the whole day as a total waste. But I have a hunch that June did some significant grieving. If she made progress toward her goal of reaching a new equilibrium, the whole day was a success."

His wife shook her head affirmatively. "I did—I really did. I feel as though I really worked through some things. I think I finally faced the reality that she isn't coming back."

Edwin sat up in his chair, looking at me in disbelief. "I'm amazed. I didn't know all that was happening. Here I was angry because I was trying to do something special and she was rejecting it. All that time something special was happening, and I wasn't aware of it."

At the end of the session Edwin thanked me for giving him a new perspective.

Perspective develops more readily when a significant amount of time lapses between our loss and the present. For that reason we can expect to gain fresh insights as the years go by. And this is a vital part of mourning.

When our son died, I thought everything I had dreamed for his life was over. In many respects that was a correct view, but other perspectives still awaited me.

As I lectured in Bakersfield, California, several years after Jeff's death, a young man said to me, "Oh, I know your son."

At first I thought he wasn't aware of Jeff's death. Maybe he had been a classmate and just hadn't kept track of what had happened to my son since their school days.

"I never met him personally, but in some respects I think I know him just as well," the young man continued. "You see, I read his poetry. So much of his person comes through to me in it."

Then he spent some time describing who my son was. His accuracy was stunning.

Five years after his death I met a college student who told me she had fastened one of Jeff's poems to her dresser mirror. She described it as "awesome" (see epilogue).

When I taught several classes at the seminary Jeff was attending at the time of his death, the students and faculty quietly shared with me how his life was still touching theirs.

These experiences forced me to develop a new perspective. Physical death does not halt all that life entails. The Scriptures mention that a person's work follows him or her after death.

During the years after a loss the mind retraces the pathways of relationship. Some of those pathways get traveled hundreds of times. With each traversing we learn new lessons and review old ones. The energy invested in it returns to strengthen us to explore new pathways.

Pain is the part of mourning that many people try to avoid. But changing our perspective on pain may make the difference between cringing and growing.

Rhonda begged me to tell her how long the paralyzing pain would last. A broadside collision had killed her 18-year-old son. She had overdosed on pills to escape the pain, but now she was willing to examine the experience of pain itself.

I shared with her a new perspective on pain when I told her that losing a son threw her whole life out of balance. Just as a bike rider struggles to regain balance after hitting loose gravel, so she was struggling to regain her balance after losing the son with whom she had bonded. "Pain," I assured her, "is not to be avoided or feared. It is a clear signal that you are in the process of bringing life back to some semblance of equilibrium. Allow it to happen. Experience it to its depths. The sharpness of the pain will lessen as you fine-tune your life."

I wanted her to see that pain was not a sign of her lack of control, but instead a sign that she was achieving more and more control. I tried to convey that it was a process, not a time-limited experience.

Many grieving people see pain as negative. They search for ways to escape it, which often leads to a form of equilibrium that is far less than ideal. Changing the perspective on pain allows us time to reach the level where life is once again rewarding and productive.

When Jeff died, I lamented over all the life experiences he would miss. The pastor who spoke at the funeral said, "What a waste." Then some months later a man from New York visited us. He had scoffed at religion for years until my son came into his life. Piece by piece Jeff chipped away at his skepticism until the "blue collar skeptic" became a Christian.

This tenderhearted New Yorker changed my perspective on Jeff's premature death. The man told me that my son had done everything I did in ministry. He had buried the dead, married sweethearts, visited the sick, preached and taught the Bible, counseled the troubled, touched the lonely, and was a model for the young. Jeff had done it with all his might. He simply hadn't done it as long as I have.

What a mind-freeing perspective! Life is for living to the fullest, and my son had lived the years he had to the fullest. Of course, I wish he had had more, but I have no complaints about what he did with the years he did have. This perspective came with time and buoyed me up like wings of an eagle.

My perspective may not work for you. That's understandable. Over the years of mourning we all develop a unique set of perspectives that do make living much easier.

I met a young man in San Francisco who had invested his inheritance and then lost it. "Do you think I'm going to sink into a deep depression in later life?" he asked.

"What's your view of wealth?" I asked.

"I'll tell you how I look at money. It represents physical energy expended. The money I invested represented the energy my grandparents expended. I'm young and have lots of energy. I can expend it the same way they did and acquire more money. It's been two years, and I haven't starved yet."

His perspective was healthy and worked for him. I complimented him on facing his loss successfully.

We all develop assumptions about life and the world in which we live. I've often called it writing a life script. When we lose important parts of our assumptive world, we often discover that our perspectives have problems in them. But we don't know that until we actually experience the loss.

My father took me to town to see the Halloween parade. I ran down to the curb and was pleased to have a front-row view of the band and the floats. Until then I had assumed that people at parades respect obvious boundaries. But I was in for a rude awakening. When the parade came by, tall people stood in front of me to get a close-up view. Souvenir sales people walked between me and the marching bands. Since I was just a kid, my stature couldn't overcome the flaws in my assumptions about parade behavior.

My father changed my perspective for me when he hoisted me up on his shoulders. Then I watched that parade with satisfaction.

Losing necessitates a gradual shift in our assumptive world. The heart of that shift is the formation of new perspectives. Time is the crucial element that hoists us up on the shoulders of alternative insights.

Chapter Seven

Secondary Loss

Andrew grieved over the death of his wife of 40 years but felt certain that he had adjusted to her not being there. Six months had gone by, and he cried only infrequently. Associating with his male friends at the coffeeshop every morning was once again part of his morning ritual. To his way of thinking he had grieved well.

Shortly after the six-month mark he met a charming Southern belle who soon became his second bride. They moved to her home in a Southern clime. His family was happy for him and positive that the new couple would be content in each other's company.

The first week in his new home was a shock for Andrew. Nell was outgoing and gregarious. Her noisy friends stopped by frequently. Twice a week she joined her friends for bridge.

After a couple weeks of social round-robin, Andrew took a walk by himself. Why was he so miserable? Why so restless? He sat on a park bench for a long time and engaged in serious introspection.

Sadness overwhelmed him as his mind recalled his quiet first wife who was content to be alone. The two of them spent many hours reading, working in their flower garden, or listening to peaceful music. A few old friends stopped to visit occasionally, but they were gentle folk who were comfortable with silence. Andrew wanted to keep this tranquil social arrangement.

Mealtimes for him were a test. His new wife savored hot spicy food from south of the border. The hotter the better. Supper was often pizza delivered to the house. After many cases of indigestion, Andrew had a clear mental picture of the simple and nourishing dishes his first wife had set before him. Hungry for the colorful vegetables fresh from the garden, he had had enough of chili powder and jalapeño peppers.

Summertime in his new home was unbearable. The humidity was high, and it was hot both day and night. He began to reminisce about cool summer evenings when he and his first wife curled up together under a warm blanket. His Northern bride had been a snuggler while his new wife couldn't stand touching in the hot, sticky rooms of their Southern home. Andrew longed for his Northern home and his snuggling bed partner.

Six weeks after the wedding he left a note on the kitchen table when Nell was playing bridge at a friend's house. It read "Gone up North where I belong. Don't bother to follow me."

Aside from remarrying too soon, Andrew had not identified the losses associated with the death of his wife. Only after entering into a totally unfamiliar environment did he begin recognizing the secondary losses. Grieving for those losses and adjusting to a new marriage could not take place simultaneously, so he bailed out of the relationship.

Every loss of primary person, place, or thing presents us with associated or secondary losses. Failure to identify and grieve for the secondary losses can slow or stall the whole process of mourning itself.

I encourage grieving people to ask and answer several important questions. What does my loss mean to me? How will life be different? How is life already different now? What do I miss? What parts of the lost relationship do I miss the most? Have I reminisced about all the dimensions of the lost relationship that I can presently recall?

Secondary losses associated with the primary loss have a greater chance of being grieved for if we ask and answer these types of questions. The chances of adjusting to all secondary losses in six months to a year are very slim. Few people can pull that much material from the memory files in such a short time frame.

The years following a loss will provide situations, places, people, and things that prompt the retrieval of new secondary losses. This is one of the reasons for the subsequent, temporary upsurge of grief (STUG) mentioned earlier in this book. If we are familiar with this process, we will not be thrown off balance when we experience it.

Learning to relax enables us to recall much more about a relationship. Total body relaxation exercises reduce the adrenaline flow, making our memory files much more accessible.

I have often thought about my childhood when I was relaxed and not quite ready for sleep. For example, my mind would focus on my blue scooter. I would remember how the dashboard was fastened to the back axle with long metal pieces. When I pulled the dashboard up, it became a seat to sit on as I coasted down the barnyard hill. I saw myself zooming down that hill. Then I remembered myself painting my scooter yellow. The yellow paint chipped off the wheels in a few places. As I went down the hill the blue and yellow blurred to make a green. It had been at least 35 years since I had thought about that old scooter. My relaxed state freed the scooter from my memory bank.

This releasing of secondary losses and new implications of a loss occurs when we take time to examine it in quiet privacy. This, added to the passage of time, enables mourning to take place without hindrance.

Janet stopped by my house because sadness had overpowered her four years after her husband died. We talked about what recent changes had taken place in her life. She had gone back to nursing a few weeks before the sadness came. As we probed her return to nursing she suddenly realized why she was sad.

She had nursed her husband for several years before he died. Thus the role of nurse had augmented her other roles of wife, friend, companion, and lover. As his condition deteriorated her nursing role intensified until he died. During the initial grief and her long struggle to provide for the children still at home, she never thought about the loss of her nursing role. Four years later her return to nursing brought that secondary loss to her attention.

Now she spent a few days reminiscing and crying about the years of illness and nursing her husband. In her journal she wrote farewells to that role and the sadness lifted. She had taken one more step in mourning.

A young mother was watching her children play on the swings and slides at the city park. Always before she had loved to observe their pure childhood delight. But this particular day at the park was sad. She tried to figure it out.

That night she was telling her husband about her strong sadness at the park. As she talked, she suddenly identified the loss she was sad about.

Her mother had died when she was 8 years old, and her father relied on her to help with her younger siblings. She had household chores that kept her from playing with the neighbors after school. The freedom of childhood had ended when her mother died. Not until she watched her own children playing that day did she become aware of that loss.

Before I began working with grief support groups I spent 10 years conducting smoking-cessation classes. There is where I first discovered that people grieve for secondary losses months and years after adjusting to the primary loss. Smokers have hundreds of perceived secondary benefits to smoking. Awkward social moments, lapses in conversation flow, tight deadlines, episodes of danger and trauma, occurrences of feeling misunderstood or abused—these are just a few of the times that smoking was comforting, soothing, or relaxing.

One man had quit smoking for a year. On his way to California he drove through the desert, and boredom set in. For years he survived boredom by slowly smoking a cigarette. Now he began longing for a cigarette. He searched the glove compartment, under his seat, and in the door pockets, but to no avail. Finally he pulled off the highway, opened the trunk, and searched through the pockets of an old overcoat. One of the pockets had a hole in it. The sight of it prompted him to feel the seams of the coat. Sure enough, there at the bottom of the lining was a crumpled-up cigarette. He fished it through the hole in the pocket and held it with a viselike grip. The first major case of boredom since he had quit smoking, he now confronted the loss right there behind his car.

"I looked at that cigarette, and then I looked at my six-foot-four body and laughed. 'You fool,' I said. 'You have said goodbye to cigarettes a year ago. Now you can say goodbye to using cigarettes to get you through a boring drive.' I ground that thing into the gravel, slammed the trunk lid shut, climbed into the car, and drove away just a little taller than six feet four."

Meeting secondary losses years after a loved one dies should not push you into guilt or feelings of weakness. Instead it is a common occurrence in the process of healthy mourning. Meet it with courage and strong resolve to live the rest of your life fully. You may even feel a little taller after you've allowed the pain to happen and wept out one more farewell to what can no longer be.

Chapter Eight

The Spiritual
Sojourn

When I'm visiting a freshly bereaved person who tells me how much her faith is helping her, my own faith in a crisis often seems so small. While I don't disbelieve the individual, in the back of my mind I wonder if he or she is concealing those dark nights of doubt and skepticism when God seems far away or nonexistent.

The people who really arouse my curiosity are the Bible quoters. The funeral is barely over, and they begin reciting Scripture verses and passages from favorite devotional writers. A verse frequently quoted is "All things work together for good to them that love God." Are such individuals for real? Do they have an immunity to sorrow?

I attended a conference on grief in which a Catholic priest led a thought-provoking discussion group. He stated that loss always produces a lapse of faith in a person's belief system. He or she may carefully camouflage it by God-talk, but in the quiet moments alone a person always meets it head-on.

A few years after that conference I stood at the bedside of a beloved church leader and moral guide to many. I met him after cancer had emaciated his body and robbed his courage bank.

"I used to be a good Christian. Every day I felt God close beside me, and I spoke to Him regularly. Now whole days go by and I don't pray. I feel forsaken. I don't know how to pray anymore. When I first became sick I prayed every day, but now I don't think it makes any difference. I have lost my faith."

Because I was a stranger to him, he let down his guard and gave me entrance into his heart. In the process he taught me that saints can doubt as deeply as they believe.

After ministering to bereaved people for nearly two decades, I am convinced that my priest friend was correct.

For three years I worked in a hospital unit devoted to treating young women with eating disorders. In a weekly spirituality group we discussed the relationship between loss and faith. As we constructed a long list of the losses they experienced, it was common for a patient to add God to the list.

Most of the young women held happily-ever-after views of God that didn't harmonize with their confusing existence in destructively enmeshed families. After years of emotional and physical pain, God seemed far away and disinterested in their personal lives.

A frail teenager wept, "If only I could have back the God I knew when I was a little girl."

I shared with her the fact that adult reality often shatters our childhood concepts of God. God is the same yesterday, today, and forever, but our concepts about Him change. Our mental pictures of God are incomplete and will be necessarily challenged by the rough places in life. Giving her permission to question her view of God, I encouraged her to revise her concepts periodically as she marked off years of life.

Spiritual assumptions change slowly, especially when loss is sudden or severe. As a result, disruptions of our faith can last for years.

A little boy lay awake nights talking to God about his mother. He told God how much he needed a mother and how much he wanted her cancer to be cured. Church members told him God would heal if enough people prayed. Despite his late-night prayers, his mother died.

Years later that little boy was a grown man and having a serious conversation with me. He had quit praying after his mother died, because a God who allowed a little boy's mother to die wasn't worth talking to. However, he refused to challenge his childhood concept of God. Until he does, communication with God will be closed. If he accepts the challenge, it will still take a long time to speak as sincerely as he did in childhood.

Shortly after our son died I felt a need to clutch tightly to God, because without Him I was afraid I'd never survive. I held serious conversations with Him. Those discussions fluctuated from scoldings to apologies, from blaming God to self-blame. I constantly begged for peace. Where else would I find it?

Gradually there came what I think must have been depression. For months I had no interest in praying. I really didn't know who it was I had been speaking to for years. Months of quiet mental searching ensued. After nearly two years of mental journey, I concluded that I will never know or understand our tragedy until I see it from God's perspective. This realization has given me enough peace to enjoy pondering the mystery of the Divine. It has also allowed me to say it like it is when I pray.

Even today major questions and fresh frustrations continue to arise in relationship to Jeff's death. But I can confront God without hesitation, because I now believe He takes me seriously. I can openly share my questions and frustrations with Him.

So many aspects of life and God's sovereignty baffle me. Jeff's death still makes no sense, nor will it ever make sense. For every answer, I encounter a dozen more questions and suspect that my spirituality will always be in a state of flux. Perhaps that is a prerequisite for spiritual growth.

My conversations with others convince me that such periods of spiritual drought and gradual resurrection of faith are common. A major assault on personal beliefs will very likely continue to have lingering ripples.

Spiritual faith is no substitute for mourning, but it is an incomparable resource for experiencing it in a way that will enable us to keep growing. Acute pain in the first months of grief and subsequent temporary upsurges of grief in the years following a loss are inevitable, faith or no faith. The suggestion that faith prevents pain does not stand up under the test of grief. Many Christians tell me that going through the pain causes some lapse of faith, but ultimately faith takes on a new strength not present prior to the loss.

A missionary to Burma by the name of Eric B. Hare returned to the United States during World War II and told his stories at an old-fashioned camp meeting. I was 10 and sat on the edge of my seat, absorbing everything he said.

As the Japanese Army moved closer to Rangoon, people fled the city. Some went with vehicles loaded with most of their possessions, but the vehicles broke down or ran out of fuel, leaving the owners to walk away with a few essentials. Missionary Hare ended up with a small suitcase and his silver trumpet. Now he played his trumpet as the children sang. I proudly played my Conn cornet alongside that impressive man. The bell-like tones of his trumpet were all that remained of his Burma sojourn, but that was enough to teach a young farmboy an unforgettable lesson.

The sojourn of mourning begins with its cruel invasion of all we hold to be spiritually significant. The relentless pain and the soul-piercing questions send us scurrying for answers. Concepts once held so tenaciously drop by the wayside. Ideas once defended fiercely are no longer useful. As the journey of mourning stretches from months to years we have less spiritual baggage. All that remain are a few unshakable convictions that ring with trumpet-like clarity. They are enough for completing your sojourn and mine.

Chapter Nine

The Persistent Call of Home

A conference speaker once described his long-term mourning for his home in the Netherlands. For months he longed for the rich taste of Dutch cheese. A year after his arrival in America as he ate a sandwich with Wisconsin cheese he found himself saying to his lunch guest, "Say, this tastes a little bit like Netherlands cheese." Five years later he eagerly went to the grocery store to buy some delicious Wisconsin cheese.

His lengthy adjustment comes as no surprise to me, even though some authors minimize the negative effects of loss of home. Mobility does produce its own fallout.

I've lost count of the corporate executives who attended the bereavement support groups I conducted for 18 years. Most of them had relocated several times in a few years. Their support system disrupted, they refused to put down roots in the new places. Then the additional loss of a loved one overwhelmed them because they had no support.

A priest related his loss of home. He had spent many years in a Latin American country. As he walked through the village everyone greeted him warmly. His fellow priests and the religious teachers were his closely knit family. Two pet dogs accompanied him on his visits to parishioners. The climate was ideal, and the resort-like surroundings brought inner peace.

Then news of his father's illness prompted a transfer to a large, impersonal city in Texas. All his friends and pets were gone, and he now worked for a bishop who was all work and no play. People on the city streets were suspicious of others. Living in a tiny room with one small window, he had to drive to visit parishioners instead of walking. He became acutely aware that the move had been a dreadful mistake. After a year in the new city his father died. Now he grieved alone both for his parental home and his Latin American home. Without adequate support his work suffered. The bishop complained and the people grumbled.

I watched my father suffer the long-term effects of moving. After World War II, fire leveled the barn on the farm he rented. Bitter disappointment gripped my father when the landlord unsympathetically announced that he had no intention of rebuilding it. Broken in spirit, my parents moved us from the home where I had spent the first 12 years of my life.

The rocky soil in southern Pennsylvania constantly taxed the patience of farmers. My father broke many plowshares while preparing the fields for winter wheat. As he plowed he yearned for the familiar fields of Lebanon County.

One day I saw him walking toward my mother. It was late afternoon, and his face appeared tired and sad. In his hands he carried a broken plowshare, a fitting symbol of his spirit.

"I'm finished!" he emphatically announced as he threw the broken plowshare to the ground before my mother's feet.

Early the next morning he drove down the long lane and didn't return until after the evening milking chores were finished. Then he announced that we were moving back to Lebanon County.

It was an 85-acre farm, too small to sustain our family during a rapidly changing economy. The fire had deprived my father of the machinery he needed to farm with. Everything that had escaped the fire we sold at auction to scrape together a down payment on the farm. Now he tried to produce crops with modified horse-drawn implements pulled by a Jeep that doubled as family car. In his heart he knew he could not regain what he had before the fire.

Soon I left home, and my father walked the fields alone. The tears coursed down his cheeks as he said, "My helpers have all left home. I can't do it by myself. I must give up my dream of rebuilding. I'll put it up for sale."

Four years after the fire the aroma of freshly plowed soil no longer met his nostrils. Now he was free from the struggle.

Occasionally he visited me in Ohio. Riding with me through the rich, flat farmland on the way to my rural parishioners, he still had visions of the old farm. As we passed fields of tall corn and golden barley I could tell the loss of home still touched him deeply.

Such behavior is not mere reminiscence that comes with advancing years. It is reality. The place where we live claims a part of our life. Leaving produces feelings of disconnectedness and unwholeness.

When leaving home occurs as a result of loss through death, divorce, disaster, aging, or financial reverses, the adjustment is doubly difficult.

The husband of a friend divorced her six months after her little girl died. Along with her grief for her girl and husband came an upsurge of grief over the loss of her parental home. She longed to be a little girl in the arms of her mother in her safe girlhood home.

Knowing that her mother lived within a short driving distance, I suggested she ask her mother to take her into her mothering arms. The return home and Mother's hugs opened the floodgates. She grieved openly in the safe environment of home.

Going back home is not possible for some of us. We can return in memory, but not physically. When some untouched bit of memory comes out, we need to replay it and experience all the details. Then we can say farewell to yet another chapter of what can no longer be.

When elderly people leave home to live in a retirement center or skilled-care facilities, they need to grieve the loss of home. If they receive no visits from family, they may never adjust to its loss. Until they say farewell to living in their home as before, they will not be able to say hello to the new living area.

I was impressed by the thoughtfulness of the son of my Norwegian church member. She was living in a skilled-care facility after dwelling on the homestead for nearly 80 years. Her son came to celebrate her ninety-fifth birthday.

"Mom, I've got a special present for your birthday. It's something to decorate your room," he told her as he pulled one of his original oil paintings from a bag.

"The homestead! Oh, son, the homestead!" she cried.

Inga's shaky finger pointed to the outbuildings. She asked her son about details she had forgotten. As he shared lots of memories with her she was obviously back home again. Occasionally her son would remind Inga that their days on the farm were good, that she was a good mother, and that they couldn't go back. He was helping her to adjust to her loss of home.

I spent 14 years visiting elderly men and women who had disengaged or withdrawn from their surroundings and families. Their world had shrunk to a tiny circle in which they scarcely had enough room for themselves, let alone a visiting chaplain.

I decided to take the course of persistence. Daily I returned with various techniques of breaking through the shell of disengagement. I suspected that their withdrawal began when others withdrew from them and when departure from home was not openly discussed with family.

My persistence was rewarded many times. Warm, aged hearts opened to me after I allowed my aged friends to reminisce about their homes and bid those special places farewell.

One of my friends made a lasting impression on me. She described her wedding. Long ago (she didn't remember how long) her girlhood sweetheart carried her across the threshold of a cute little home in the hill country of Texas. She described the curtains, the furniture, the pictures on the walls, and the garden behind the house. The gate in the front yard had roses on both sides. She and her husband raised two happy children there. All was picturesque until her sweetheart died suddenly.

A few years later she had adjusted to living alone. Everything in the old house comforted her. It was like living in a gallery of yesterdays. Feebleness kept her from going upstairs and cataracts dimmed her vision. Yet the old house had smells about it that told stories from the past.

On a cool December day her son came to announce that he was taking her to live in a nice facility where she could be with other people her age. She had no choice in the matter. Her final comments in telling the story still give me pain.

"I turned to take one last look. My son told me to close the door on everything dear to me. As we drove away I looked again at the path to the front gate. I saw the door through which my husband had carried me long ago. Yes, I closed the door on a lifetime. I have longed to go back every day since."

Day after day I invited her to open the door of that little hill country home. She relived happy days and not-so-happy ones. We laughed and cried about home. I let her know how worthwhile I thought her life was.

Gradually she closed the door of her little home of her own free will. At the same time she slowly opened a door to her new world, of which I was a part.

What about the long-term effects of moving on children? Do they adjust as quickly as we think?

I know a young woman who lived through years of pain because her parents insisted on responding to different invitations to serve their church as missionaries. They sent her to a boarding school for the children of missionaries so that she lived at home only during school recess. When her parents changed jobs they bundled her off to a different boarding school. The negative results of her uprootedness received treatment only after she developed an addiction to alcohol.

When I served as chaplain in psychiatric wards, the psychiatrists on quite a few occasions asked me to labor with the parents of teenage patients. Frequent moves and absentee parenthood were often the culprits behind the emotional upheaval of these young people.

As a church employee I think I moved too frequently. It was difficult for my sons to adjust to new houses, new schools, new teachers, and new friends. In some respects loss of home extended into years, not just months. Most of the time we made the moves without consulting the boys. I will always be of the opinion that they had a right to be involved in the transfers. My wife graciously accepted my decisions, but uprooting her again and again had its negative effect also.

A year and a half after we buried our oldest son we relocated from Michigan to Texas. That trip was a trail of tears for my wife. Leaving the resting place of her own flesh and blood was a cruel excision of her identity. Her pain did not end when we glimpsed the skyline of Fort Worth for the first time.

Experiencing loss of home personally and observing similar

losses in the lives of both young and old have prompted bits of advice that I share when people ask me about moving. Here are a few of the suggestions I make:

1. Don't move unless you have to.

2. Try to have as many choices in the move as you can. This gives you some control and makes the adjustment smoother.

3. Don't move abruptly. Try to gain plenty of time to assimilate the change into your thinking.

4. Plan to stay in communication with friends. Make some trips back to see them. Arrange for your friends to visit you in your new environment.

5. Allow enough time to go to the new place before you make the move. Get acquainted with the area. Shop in the stores, find a barber, locate your bank, read the newspaper, visit the school, check out the library. Make the new area your home before you move there.

6. Begin developing a support system as soon as you arrive. Don't wait until you feel like doing it. Put your social foot forward with realistic expectations.

7. Decorate your new home as soon as you unpack the boxes—or sooner, if possible. Plant flowers and your favorite variety of tree in the front yard. Find a new picture to hang on a sunny wall. Let the sun shine into each room. Never darken your new home with shades and heavy drapes. Light is essential to ward off depression.

8. Spend as much time outdoors as you can. Becoming intimate with the soil and the growing plants in your new area ties you to the place.

9. Deliberately say many small farewells to the old homestead before moving. It makes it easier to say small hellos to the new home.

10. Count on periodic down days. When they come, make contact with an old friend. Catch up on the news. An increase in the phone bill is better than spending a gray day alone.

Chapter Ten

Echoes of Divorce

Heather sat on the edge of her chair, her legs swinging nervously. At 8 years of age she had a big pack to carry. She came to see me because her mother and father had divorced eight months earlier. Her big brown eyes sparkled with tears during our 40-minute session.

"You sure have a lot of sadness inside of you," I commented. "Do you know why your mother and father divorced?"

Her legs swung faster and the tears dropped on the collar of her pretty dress. She looked down at her knees and pointed her index finger at herself.

"Did you make them divorce?" I asked.

She shook her head up and down as she broke into a sob. At that point there were two teary faces in the room. I had to share her pain.

During the next few months Heather and I examined her reasons for assuming that she had been the downfall of the marriage. An intelligent girl, she was able to think things through pretty carefully. She assured me that she no longer blamed herself, but somewhere in my heart I keep asking myself if Heather still struggles with guilt.

Alan was a responsible entrepreneur at age 20 and managed his own lawn care business in a large Texas city. The whole enterprise was a futile attempt to win his father's approval. He never succeeded in getting the nod of approval from the man he admired.

Divorce entered the picture, and now Alan's father lived with a new bride about his son's age. One day Alan jumped into his shiny new lawn care truck and headed to his father's new home. Leaping over the privacy fence, he entered the kitchen from the open back door. Patiently he waited for his father to come home.

No sooner had the father seen his son sitting in the kitchen than he exploded into a volley of angry words. "This is not your home, and you have no right to come here without an invitation, do you understand that? Now get in that rig of yours and beat it before Kathy comes back."

Alan never had a chance to show off his new truck, the symbol of his success in business. He decided that his father would never see him or his truck. Two years after this incident Alan was still searching for ways to live without his father's approval.

Eric and his wife attended a grief support program I conducted. The constant verbal stabs June gave him during the sessions puzzled me. For a couple in their 50s they seemed to have an unusual amount of resentment between them.

"This man worries me sick," June told the group. "Our son being electrocuted was enough for me to bear without worrying about Eric every day. I never know whether he's going to walk through the kitchen door from one day to the next. He can't take on jobs that are safe—he has to live in danger all the time. Working as an officer in the special police was bad enough, but now he's into skydiving and who knows what next. He makes me nervous all the time."

"Well, I need to say something to defend June in front of this group. She has reason to say the things she just said. It all started when I was about 12. My folks broke up. That's when I decided I had to be tough to survive. I joined the boxing club in town and from that day to this I have been boxing. When I was in high school I fought 40 matches and had 18 knockouts. I fought my way through rejection and bitterness, and I'm still fighting. The rougher the better. Now, I know that upsets June, but that's been my way of surviving."

Eric and June saw a therapist for nearly a year before he got the life-shattering effects of his parents' divorce in some semblance of control.

In 1977 Dr. James J. Lynch wrote *The Broken Heart—Medical Consequences of Loneliness.* He opened his book with a comment about how our modern culture nurtures the belief that love is a word without meaning. "A whole generation of detached, independent, self-sufficient, non-committed individuals agree . . . that no one really needs to get hurt in modern human relationships. You can be intimate with someone and then leave, and nothing bad will happen" (*The Broken Heart—Medical Consequences of Loneliness* [New York: Basic Books, 1977]).

Eric, Alan, and Heather can testify that this widespread philosophy is a lie. Divorce leaves people drained emotionally, socially, physically, and often financially. Strewn on the path from divorce court to home alone are resentment, rejection, hatred, total shock, and uncertainty.

My heart goes out to the children of divorce. Five years of teaching school cemented my resolve to save every marriage I can.

Lynch maintains that the death or absence of parents in early childhood is a contributing factor in premature death from all causes. He believes that we do not yet fully understand the effect of divorce on children. But society still fosters the illusion that children are highly resilient when it comes to the damage of divorce.

Archibald Hart wrote, "Divorce, although no longer the stigma it once was, is nevertheless a wrenching, painful, unfortunate series of events that imposes on children adjustments and changes they often are not capable of making. The effects of divorce are far more serious and long-lasting than most divorced parents are willing to admit to themselves" (*Children and Divorce* [Waco, Tex.: Word Books, 1982]).

Hart describes his own experience of having divorced parents. His adjustment took years. He still wonders whether his life would have been happier had his parents worked out their problems. He suspects that what emerged from his situation is still only second-best.

Adult children of divorced parents struggle with serious losses of dreams. Taking children to Grandma's and Grandpa's house for holidays and vacations is a significant treat for both the children and the grandchildren. But divorce makes this impossible.

Security in the mind of children has close ties to the marriage integrity of their parents. That security carries over from childhood into adulthood. The strong marriage of parents provides a model for children that serves as hope for their own future marital happiness. Divorce sends tremors through the whole sense of security.

A close friend of mine feels a low-grade sorrow about her divorced parents that never goes away. Special holidays and anniversaries stir her sorrow and emotionally color many important events in her life.

Divorce affects our lives in many ways. They include:

DIALOGUE

My wife and I met a mutual friend who had gone through a divorce about five years ago. Chatting nonstop with a bright, almost too optimistic tone, the woman made frequent references to her counselor's amazement at her progress. In a few minutes we heard all about her great journeys to faraway enchanted places. It seemed too good to be true. My wife and I agreed that our friend was still struggling with the long-term effects of divorce.

One of the reasons it takes a long time to upright yourself after a capsized marriage is that it has interrupted normal dialogue. Dialogue takes time to develop in a marriage, and it takes time to reconstruct it after the marriage ends.

Such dialogue is more than sharing things with another person. It is opening up yourself so completely that a part of you meshes with the other person while at the same time part of the other person fuses with you. It is entering into the pain and joy of another human being.

Dialogue involves both verbal and nonverbal communication and communion and is a gradual process. When divorce ends dialogue, it produces a vacuum that can last for many months.

Dr. James J. Lynch emphatically states that living dialogue is the elixir of life. "Dialogue consists of reciprocal communication between two or more living creatures. It involves the sharing of thoughts, physical sensations, ideas, ideals, hopes, and feelings."

A slow erosion of dialogue usually precedes divorce. The deterioration is often so subtle that the couple do not notice any appreciable change until one day the relationship comes to a screeching halt.

Many divorced persons then embark on a long search for lost dialogue, a journey that sometimes lasts for years. They devote their total energy to detecting and nourishing little signs of hope. Should all signs of restoration vanish, they may spend their reserve energies lashing out and verbally slaying the ex-spouse.

Calvin picked up his two children every Friday evening. One week his ex-spouse, Sue, had had an unusually difficult time at work. When he was ready to leave with the children, she leaned her head on his shoulder and sighed, "Oh, am I glad to see you! This day has been the pits!"

That's all Calvin needed. His mind raced straight to the altar. He was sure Sue was ready to reconcile, but his search for lost dialogue had caused him to jump to conclusions. Her gesture was one of mere exasperation, not a desire to restore intimacy.

Attempts to recover lost dialogue sometimes will get rewarded early in the troubled relationship, but as time elapses the chances become slimmer. At some point you have to face reality and channel your energies into beginning dialogue with others.

BAGGAGE CARRIERS

I conducted a divorced persons' support group for 12 people who had passed the point of hoping for reconciliation and renewed dialogue. They spent the first three sessions in angry reviews of past hurts. At the close of the third session I called a moratorium on further venting.

During the next three sessions we restricted our time to restructuring the present, using personal strengths as the building blocks. A young mother who had experienced exacerbated symptoms of a chronic illness since her divorce reaped especially large dividends from that change of focus. It relieved her of the increased pain. Once again she could care for her two children and enjoy a few activities with them.

We looked back on those first three weeks and jokingly called what went on "baggage carrying." The people in the group realized that it's natural to react to divorce with sadness, anger, defensiveness, fear, guilt, and disappointment. Such reactions spontaneously arise even before we have time to think about them. However, whether we embrace or drop them is up to us.

We can rehearse our injuries hundreds of times and experience the negative feelings and reactions over and over. That way we get lots of mileage out of our loss and wear down the tread on the rest of our lives.

Judy Tatelbaum recommends getting through painful experiences quickly and easily by "living them moment to moment. This means feeling pain when we feel pain and then letting it go, being angry when we are angry and then letting it go, and the same with any of our feelings" (*You Don't Have to Suffer* [New York: Harper and Row, 1989]).

Divorce holds the potential for lingering pain that defies a person to put it away. I am acquainted with people who have been crippled by their injuries for years. In spite of counseling and support groups their paralysis continued. Living a productive and rewarding life seemed an impossibility. In the meantime their personal turmoil brought on a variety of physical and emotional illnesses.

DENIAL

For the past 18 years I have been presenting seminars on loss and living with loss. Seldom have I finished such a seminar without one or more persons talking to me about their pending divorce. The scenarios are always similar.

The divorce proceedings are nearly finalized. Their divorcing spouse is seeing another person, but they are not able to believe it is over. Quite a few of them have been reading books written by authors who insist that you can save any marriage if you pray hard enough. Attempts at counseling have been made, sometimes for years, but the proceedings are still going ahead full steam.

In some instances the divorce is final, but the person wants to believe that the new relationship will fail and then he or she can renew the marriage. One man I encountered had been banking on such a renewal for five years. In the meantime he had put his life on hold. The enormous investment of emotional energy in such wishful thinking and planning had taken its toll on his emotional and physical health.

I always make it very clear to couples in conflict that with intense effort they can make their marriage work. With the power that God so freely offers there is no reason the marriage has to end. But I also let them know that it takes hard work on both sides of the relationship. When one partner refuses to invest in restructuring the relationship, there comes a point when the other spouse needs to face reality and begin a new chapter in life.

REBUILDING WITH GOD

Describing the prolonged pain people experience after divorce is impossible. I have listened to men and women pour out their feelings for hours, but I find it beyond my power to capture their hurt feelings into a paragraph or two. And I confess to having feelings of helplessness as I see the intense sorrow and injury that makes their faces look old before their time. Their slumping bodies and shocking list-lessness are so apparent that I often can't get it out of my mind for days afterward. Seeing these manifestations linger for years has sent me looking for answers to dealing with the problems they cause.

Lately I've been amazed at the rapid changes in social behavior, moral values, negative use of technology, and the increasing disre-spect for the feelings of others. Daily we witness unbelievably vio-lent crime, terrorism, megadeath, weakening of links between parents and children, and the continual breaking of bonds between husbands and wives. The potential for complicated mourning has skyrocketed to the point where grief specialists wonder if anything can ever resolve some of these complicated losses.

Western society has come face-to-face with heartbreak far be-yond the capacity of our healing arts. I believe our only hope for a restored, healthy equilibrium is complete reliance on God. My expe-rience has convinced me that for the life-altering pain of divorce, di-vine intervention is an indispensable healing element.

My pastoral colleagues and I frequently meet people crippled by divorce. Such individuals have been to many therapists, but they still find themselves immobilized by their injuries. Now they come to pastors and other clergy because everything else has failed. They ask if God might have some solutions.

When I think back on my experiences with such individuals, I find myself agreeing with the Christian psychiatrist John White, who said, "Christianity has not been tried and found wanting—it has been found but not really tried, even by the churches. Only an emascu-lated, gutless travesty of it has been tried" (*Putting the Soul Back in Psychology* [Downers Grove, Ill.: InterVarsity Press, 1987]).

Men, women, and children with broken spirits can indeed find true healing when they open the inner sanctum of their soul to the presence of the life-giving, peace-giving Lord.

A young mother described her inner pain caused by years of re-jection and abuse. She feared she was slipping over the edge into the nightmare of despair. Somehow she had to find a cure for the injuries of the past.

"You have been to many human healers without success," I told her. "Now you come to me. I cannot heal you, but I want to intro-duce you to my Friend who can. His name is Jesus. Because He made you in your mother's womb, He knows you better than you do yourself. Now He is waiting for you to come to Him for healing."

"How do I do that?" she asked.

"Speak to Him in the quiet of your bedroom or in a favorite peaceful place. Tell Him in simple words that you have tried to heal your pain but all your efforts have failed. Then say that you are giving your pain to Him to cast into the ocean of His grace. Explain that you are now ready to receive His peace and His purpose for your life. Every day after that, thank Jesus for taking your pain away and for giving you peace and purpose."

She seemed noticeably relieved after I invited her to give her pain to Jesus. "I love God very much," she said. "I've been wondering if He could help me, so I'm going to do what you said. I really feel good about it."

Experiencing pain fully as it comes, then giving it to Jesus so that you can live beyond it—that's a powerful cure.

A patient in the hospital was carrying tons of emotional baggage from the past. The pain was crippling him. One night he had a serious conversation with God.

"You know, God, I've felt my sorrow to the depths. There's nothing else I can do about it. Right now I'm giving all this pain to You because You know what to do with it. I'm asking You for strength so I can go home quickly and care for my family."

A month later he wrote me a letter and reported that he and his family had begun a new life together.

Giving our pain to God is not hocus-pocus. Rather, it is healing that He has just waiting for His crippled children to tap into.

John White says, "Churches have stopped believing in divine power, paying only lip service to it. So they no longer can call on it in an hour of need. All they can do is warn us away from the dangers of getting too close to anything miraculous. God may be all-powerful, but it is the Devil we must really look out for!"

It is a sad day when the fortress of strength—the church—becomes a place of doubt and uncertainty. But the power of the gospel has not changed. The church need not make any apologies for directing hurting people to God for restoration.

I have not experienced the pain of divorce. My pain has come from disillusionment with church leaders that I looked up to for an example. It has been caused by the loss of loved ones, including my oldest son. And I could add to it pain connected to awkward times during adolescence.

But I have also experienced the restoration of peace and purpose from God. My simple request and ongoing prayer of thanks started the rebuilding with God that will probably continue the rest of my life. I know that God can and does heal any pain.

What could have ended up in chronic bitterness and rage at God and others has now been turned into a strong conviction that life is for living. As a result, joy comes to me and to those I live with.

Given the certainty of divine power over the pain of the past, I can agree with Judy Tatelbaum when she says that loss and pain are inevitable, but suffering is our choice. "Suffering is perpetuating the pain of the past and carrying it into the future." The choice not to suffer is not something made and kept through the personal power of the survivor of divorce. Rather, that power to choose life is God's gift to us.

Chapter Eleven

Slow-fading Regrets

A football player watches the reruns of the strategic plays of a crucial game. It's a year after his team lost the championship, but he's still going over the contest in his mind. He's still kicking himself for calling the play that proved to be the deciding factor. His team made plenty of good plays that season, but that particular one dies slowly in his memory. His team lost the championship, and he'll never have a chance to make that play different.

Alice's disabled husband begged her to stay home, but work at the factory had picked up to seven days a week. In her usual rush that morning she gave a quick see-you-later call as she left by the garage door. After work she stopped at a few shops, but something troubled her. Suddenly she felt an overwhelming urge to get back home. Her screams broke the stony silence of the house as she found him dressed in her nightgown, his last desperate attempt at closeness with her before he died.

For many years Alice replayed that dreadful day. Although she tried every alternative, her mental replays didn't change her loss. Did she spend time being close to him? Yes. Did she fail to spend time with him? Yes. The cruel mental games went on, intensely at first, then subsiding slowly over the years.

My friend Arlyn never learned to express feelings comfortably. When he married he told himself that he'd be warm and expressive to his wife and children, but his intentions never became reality. His wife was hospitalized for treatment of depression, his parents died, and a freak accident killed his grandchild. Arlyn considered his adjustment normal because he never broke down and cried. He was not aware that the rest of his family also followed his pattern of grieving. They kept everything to themselves. After the death of the grandchild the family seemed to fall apart. Communication ceased as they all pretended the loss had not occurred.

During a very low period Arlyn stopped to chat with me about his deep sorrow that did not seem to go away. When I asked him how he handled strong feelings, he rehearsed his total failure at being warm and expressive. He was convinced that he had emotionally robbed his family and caused the disintegration of its closeness. The regrets had been plaguing him for a long time. Finally his self-torture brought him to an emotional valley that seemed too deep to escape.

Although he asked God to forgive him for being so cold with his family, he couldn't forgive himself. I suggested that he look in a full-length mirror and have a conversation with himself.

"Arlyn, you have been unable to share important feelings with your family," he should say to himself. "You are not perfect. But I am forgiving you for not being perfect. I am forgiving you for being cold."

Then I suggested that he take each member of his family to brunch, after which he would openly admit his lack of perfection and ask for forgiveness.

Arlyn discovered that self-forgiveness liberated him to love and to express love. Shortly after he dropped the baggage of self-blame he visited one of his daughters. Making eye contact with her, he said, "Sally, I have not shared feelings with you very much during your years of growing up. It has made it difficult for you to adjust to Marty's death. I'm very sorry. I ask you for forgiveness. I'm very proud of you and your accomplishments despite my coldness. I love you very much. You're important to me, and I appreciate you."

The daughter didn't know how to respond to his unexpected expression. She had never dealt with such honest affirmation before, and Arlyn knew that she was stunned. But he felt alive in a way he had never been before.

Regrets can linger like a nagging cough, disrupting your peace of mind and ability to live in the present. They do not disappear quickly, but persist until you take them firmly in hand and put them in their place.

The day my son died such regrets invaded my thinking. I remember taking a walk to a little park near my home where I sat down on an old picnic table and began reviewing my record as a father to Jeff. Incident after incident plunged wildly into my mind. The time I spanked him for throwing an onion through the back door window. Not teaching him to check the fluid levels in the old Buick and then scolding him for not checking the oil when he filled the gas tank. Failing to sense his strong desire to learn to drive the secondhand Toyota I bought. Would the regrets ever stop screaming at me?

This deluge of regrets had first swept over me the day he died. The pain was too great to keep on bearing. Finally I decided to take the regrets to God. "Kind Lord, I've been a failure to my son so many times. I can't change any of that now. I can't talk to Jeff about it. All I can do now is ask You to forgive me for the times I failed him. Forgive me for being a poor father."

I believe that God then prompted me to engage in another type of self-examination by that picnic table. It was this second phase of the examination that provided the balance that enabled me ultimately to forgive myself.

"Kind Lord," I cried, "there were times You helped me to be a good father. We had time to hike, camp, and backpack together. We shared deep religious thoughts that were often beyond my comprehension. Long, late-night struggles over his choice of lifework were shared with not the slightest wish for them to end. I told him that whatever he decided to do I would be there for him. When he was growing up I took him with me many places. I loved him, and I let him know that. There were many times I was a good father because You helped me to be there for Jeff. I thank You for the times I was a good father."

I wish I could tell you that my picnic table encounter ended the regrets. It didn't. Even more of them haunted me. Over the years I have had to tell myself repeatedly that it is not fair to judge my past life by what I now understand about being a father. I have had to admit my lack of perfection and forgive myself for being the flawed person that I am. And in the back of my mind I have had to settle the fact that I would need to forgive myself freely many times in the future. But I told myself that if God forgives more than 70 times seven, why should I not grant multiple pardons to myself?

Carrying the weight of yesterday's mistakes will only prevent you from experiencing today's positive happenings. Helping to ease the burden of a fellow life traveler is impossible when your own hands are full of your own regrets. Of course, you'll face the regrets again, but that doesn't mean you have to pick them voluntarily.

As I was waiting in line to buy a bus ticket one day my attention riveted on the passenger at the head of the line. He had a suitcase that was bulging and splitting. Old socks and shirts stuck out all over the place. The ticket agent was shaking his head, but the old man who owned the suitcase continued to plead. Finally the agent took the suitcase from the man and placed it on a table behind the counter. With a huge roll of tape he secured that overstuffed luggage and tied a shipping label to the handle. Ticket in hand, the elderly gentleman made his way to the waiting bus.

Overstuffed suitcases slow things down and can keep us from catching the bus. They may be a sign of trying to hang on to possessions we should have discarded a long time ago. Some of the items taking up space in our emotional suitcases are "If only I hadn't," "If only I had," and "If only I had done more." If you have overpacked the suitcase of your mind with regrets, why not ask a good friend to help you dump the unnecessary baggage? Why not travel lighter so you can enjoy the rest of the trip?

Chapter Twelve

Chronic Painmakers

My brother Bill occasionally asked me to help him with farmwork. He was a sharecropper near the Susquehanna River in southern Pennsylvania. One day we drove down to the river to buy groceries from a little country store. As I sat in the car waiting for him, I heard strange singing. "Tommie tike a vick. Tommie tike a vick." Over and over came the odd sounds set to music. A few minutes later I saw a large man with a big smile on his face walking with an awkward gait toward the car. I noticed that his head was unusually large for the rest of his body. Passing the car, he disappeared over a bank leading to the boat docks.

I was 12 years old and couldn't figure out what was the matter with him. Bill later told me that the man—who was named Tommie—had been born with a problem that would keep him childlike for the rest of his life. "Whatever you do, don't make fun of him. He's a very kind person. His folks love him very much. They'd be upset if they heard anyone making fun of their son."

Eventually I had time to play among the boats while Bill went fishing with his hired man. Tommie's job was to clean the boats and tie them to the dock. I listened to his happy songs and talked with him. While I seldom understood what he was saying, I always felt his affection for me and looked forward to spending time with him whenever my brother took me to his farm.

At the age of 12 I never thought about how Tommie's parents felt about him. It wasn't until I met Darla that I sensed what might have happened in the quiet of Tommie's home.

Darla carried her tiny baby girl in a little basket lined with lamb's wool. Jessica was 1 year old when I first saw her, and weighed only five pounds. The mother explained that the child had a chromosome disorder that would limit her life span to no more than 6 years. Jessica would never sit up on her own, never talk, and never grow any larger. The mother had been to many experts hoping to hear a more promising prognosis, but they all told her the same thing.

She came to see me every other week for several years because talking about her child's problem at home had begun to strain her marriage. It was during these many months that I learned something about the unending pain and grief of parents who have children with special needs.

"Going shopping infuriated me. People stared and asked stupid questions. One lady had the nerve to ask me why I don't feed my baby. Doesn't she know that Jessica will never be chubby like healthy babies? I got to the place where I stayed in my house and made my husband do the shopping. I was a prisoner in my house all because ignorant people made it too painful to go out."

"How long did you withdraw?" I asked.

"There are times when I still hide, but just a few weeks ago I decided I was not going to be a prisoner because of stupid people. I decided to be more assertive. Now when people stare I look at them and tell them about Jessica's condition. When they ask dumb questions, I fill them in on what her situation is. Now the clerks know us. We chat about Jessica instead of enduring uncomfortable silence."

I asked Darla how long it took for her to admit to herself that Jessica would never grow to adulthood.

"By the time I heard the third specialist's prognosis I told myself that Jessica would never make it to 6. That was fine, but then these people from all kinds of agencies asked to come to the house. They told me about exercise programs and nutrition supplements that they were sure would help. I'd get excited and almost hopeful. Then I'd go to another specialist to get another opinion. Finally I decided I would not put my emotions on any more roller coasters. I refused to have any more visits from any organization."

"Do you have any conflicting emotions?" I inquired.

"Oh, you better believe I do. Some evenings I put Jessica to bed and pray to God that she will die in her sleep. Then in the morning when I find her alive I cry out loud and thank God that my little Jessica is alive."

One day about two years after Darla began her visits to my office, she gently tube-fed Jessica, carefully placed her in the little basket, and set the basket and baby on the top of the file cabinet. I could tell she had been crying. With some prodding she told me about her heartache.

"Sometimes I lie in bed at night and think about Jessica. I cry because she will never be able to play with other children. She won't learn to read. We'll never bake cookies together and pick out pretty clothes at the store. My little Jessica has been robbed of so much that life is all about. Instead, it is one crisis after another. Time after time she has a seizure, and I rush her to the hospital. The poor little child doesn't deserve this."

But other times Darla was much more upbeat. "This little munchkin gets to my heart. My family think I'm seeing things, but I kid you not. Jessica has her own little ways of smiling and expressing her love. There are special moments in the early hours of the morning. As I am rocking her we commune together. I know she won't grow up like other kids, but she has become a very important part of my life. I am amazed at what this little girl does for me. She may have a mountain of problems, but she is doing what God put her here to do."

By the time Jessica was 3, Darla began teaching classes for mothers with special children. The child accompanied her as she went to elementary and junior high schools to talk to students about how to treat children with special needs. Darla felt good about her progress.

"What about your marriage?" I asked one day.

"There are times when Art wants nothing to do with Jessica. That's when I get angry and don't want anything to do with him. Other times he makes over Jessica, and I catch him talking to her. That's when I feel close to him, and we have a honeymoon all over again. He is working hard at the business and is always tired when he comes home, so I try not to bother him. He's a good man. I tell him so. What do you expect when your only child is not the child you dreamed of having? We have decided that after Jessica is gone we'll still have each other, so we go out, just the two of us. Not often, but enough to stay close."

Every week I commended Darla for taking time for herself. I

gradually realized how totally focused on the child a parent can become. At times Darla apologized for coming to my office so long, but I kept telling her that needing a support system for years is not unusual when chronic loss is involved.

An employment opportunity opened up on the West Coast for Art. Together Darla and I managed the farewells to scores of helping persons. After arranging for medical support in the new community before they moved, she promised me that she would find ways to educate the community about the needs of special children.

Shortly after Jessica's fourth birthday she died in her sleep. A letter from Darla told me that she was grateful for the many contributions her daughter had made to her life and the lives of hundreds of other people. At the same time she acknowledged the constant upsurges of grief. She was fully aware that she would be handling additional chapters of mourning in the years to come.

Randy stopped by my office with a big problem. Five years earlier his son had been paralyzed. Jud had been at the age when backpacking and fishing were big on the father-son agenda. The two of them had been into outdoor activities. About the same time as Jud's misfortune a new baby had joined the family. Now that newborn was 5 years old. She would try to snuggle up to her father, but Randy pushed her away. Seldom picking her up, he avoided close contact with his daughter. Many times the little girl cried and told her mother that Daddy didn't love her.

"I can't go on breaking my little girl's heart, but for some reason I can't bring myself to be kind to her," he explained to me.

"I want to talk about Jud," I told him. "When you think of him, what goes through your mind?"

"I see a husky kid with a fishing rod in his hand or a pack on his back."

"Do you see a boy who cannot walk?"

"No. I don't want to see that. In fact, I don't go into his room unless I am forced to do so. I can't bear to go on vacations, because I'd have to be around him too much. I see a healthy boy climbing mountains and riding a trail bike."

"Randy, the boy you see in your mind does not exist any longer. Jud is not going to climb mountains again. He will not go fishing and backpacking with you. That Jud is gone. There is a new Jud in that room you avoid. I know it is painful, but you must go into his room every morning and say goodbye to that robust young man in your mind. Then you'll be able to say hello to all the potential accomplishments in his life. You can be a part of those new chapters in Jud's life if you say farewell to the dreams you have for him, dreams that cannot come true."

"But what about my girl? I came to see you about her."

"Right now let's concentrate on Jud. I have a hunch that you can't say hello to Jud in his paralyzed condition until you say goodbye to the Jud who went hiking with you five years ago. Perhaps your clinging to the former Jud has made it difficult to open your arms to your little girl. Right now, why not try to identify and accept the real Jud?"

It has been quite a few years since Randy bid farewell to the former Jud. A close relationship has developed between him and both his children. At times Jud's paralysis still colors Randy's attitude toward the children, but his understanding of the far-reaching effects of loss enables him to put those attitudes into perspective.

Chronic illness causes ongoing grief that affects not only the person with the disease but also her or his family. My work in cancer wards and hospices over the past 20 years has provided me the opportunity to guide people through the confusing maze of mourning that doesn't seem to have an end.

Cal organized the volunteer fire and rescue squad in his township, but now he could do nothing but listen to the police band on the radio next to his hospital bed. Multiple sclerosis left him stiff and unable to do so much as scratch his nose. His buddies from the fire and rescue squad no longer visited, and his two sons had quit coming. They had not seen Cal in two years, preferring to remember him the way he used to be.

Only one person was left. His wife came every day at precisely 11:00 in the morning. If she was a few minutes late, he would slip into a state of panic.

Usually Cal was in an agreeable mood, but he was not good at sharing his feelings with anyone. As his frustration increased, the nurses became the target of his anger. That's when I was called to his bedside. I confronted him with his behavior and suggested that maybe the two of us could talk man-to-man. Cal talked and cried while I wiped away his tears with facial tissue.

Outraged when I learned that his fire and rescue buddies had deserted him, I wrote a letter to the squad and suggested that they might visit Cal. One day he caught me off guard. "Larry, you called or wrote to the squad, didn't you?"

"Yes, I did. Why?"

"Larry, don't go to bat for me. I have to stand in the batter's box alone. You can't hit the ball for me. I've been fighting MS for quite a few years, and I've struck out many times. A lot of people rooted for me down through the years, but people get tired and some of them forget. When it comes right down to it, Larry, God will get me through this rough spot. And if everyone finds it too painful to stick around, God will be with me."

The nurses and I decided that we would make it a threesome—Cal, God, and us. We would be a part of Cal's support system. Becoming family for him, we laughed and joked and shared our family events. Soon Cal looked forward to each new day to see his friends. We were happy that we did not allow him to withdraw into himself.

Chronic disease brings unrelenting grief that we have to deal with as it comes, but withdrawal has devastating effects. Both the ill person and the family need the steady support of a caring community.

Several researchers have found that family members adjust to a cancer death of a loved one more easily when the chronic illness lasts from six to 18 months (Therese A. Rando, *Treatment of Complicated Mourning* [Champaign, Ill.: Research Press, 1993], p. 508). Their finding coincides with the observations made by my associates in hospice care. Our conversations with family members reveal that in less than six months the family doesn't have enough time to assimilate the possibility of death. Their hopes for recovery remain very high. Many of them are still exploring a variety of treatment approaches. They do not yet have time for anticipatory grieving. Yet many of these families experience prolonged grief similar to what one would expect to see after sudden loss.

When illness lasts longer than 18 months, however, we notice several factors that could contribute to prolonged grief. Some families build up fresh denial in light of the sick person's ability to go through several regressions and remissions. Frequently we hear people say, "She'll lick this thing yet." Families who do much of the caregiving themselves become physically and emotionally exhausted, which appears to worsen the situation. Seeing a loved one suffer and deteriorate physically fills the mind with images that crowd out any active grieving. And any sense of relief when death does come only produces guilt that may last for months.

Families who have cared for a loved one for a long time become deeply emotionally involved in the situation. Withdrawing all that emotional energy takes time. In addition to this is the career-like routine of caregiving. After the death there seems to be a vacuum. I've heard people say, "I don't know what to do with myself. I'm bored sometimes." Another frequent comment is "I worked so hard to get Mother well, but she died just the same. At times I wonder if I did enough for her."

Families who lose a member after a lengthy illness need both immediate and long-term support. This support should include sharing information about the nature of grief and how to avoid the negative effects of complicated mourning. Such families need nonjudgmental people who will listen and not tire of hearing the same stories told repeatedly. These supportive people should be steady friends who are not reticent to speak about the loss. They should also nudge the family to reengage in the normal activities of life.

During a long illness families assume and assign roles that get them through the crisis, but perpetuating those roles may not be healthy after the crisis ends. A supportive friend will encourage the family to reassess the parts they have been filling.

Practical support should include such things as mowing the lawn, housecleaning, and child care, and should continue for a year or more.

Thoughts, memories, and feelings linger for years. But the mourner will often not mention them for fear of being misunderstood. Such suffering in silence only extends and intensifies the pain. Open expression and analysis of these lingering reactions is vital to healthy mourning.

The various caregivers that I am associated with report a high number of people coming to them for help because of the strain that accompanies chronic illness in the family. One particular experience especially stands out in my mind.

For three years a woman called me on the phone to talk about her husband, who had been diagnosed as having Alzheimer's disease. She didn't dare leave the house for fear of what he would do while she was gone. Each phone call reported a subtle loss of the man's personhood. We would reminisce about how she had enjoyed that part of Carl in the past, and then I helped her to say farewell to that aspect of his personality. After three years of many farewells Carl became violent, and Mary admitted him to a veterans' hospital.

For the next several months she struggled with guilt caused by the fact that she felt relieved to have him out of the house. Simultaneously she began to develop a social life of her own. After Carl died, Mary worked hard at regaining her equilibrium, but it took five years from the time of the diagnosis to do so. That's a long grief.

Mary taught me that anticipatory grief is not necessarily grieving a person's death before she or he dies. It is grieving for little losses that show up between the diagnosis and the death. Talking, weeping, and saying farewell to skiing together, going to church together, and dozens of other facets of togetherness is what anticipatory grief is all about. For some people this period can last for years.

I firmly believe that whenever circumstances permit, the ill person and the family should acknowledge that a chronic disease exists, put affairs in order, and then get on with life. Life is for living and is short for all of us. Why waste precious time focusing on only the disease and possible death?

Jack was a hardworking physician. Both he and his wife, Audrey, began to notice that he was not as strong and active as he used to be. Within a month he lost weight and couldn't work more than a few hours a day. He and Audrey went to a large medical center and had a battery of tests run. While they waited for the results they celebrated their thirty-fifth wedding anniversary as best they could.

The next day the medical center receptionist ushered them into a tiny interview room. The physician walked into the room with Jack's chart open in his hand. "Very interesting case. Very interesting case. I really don't think there is anything we can do for you here. You can read the report, Jack. There is no cure for your condition."

Jack told me, "I couldn't believe this was a doctor. He never prepared me for the bad news, and left the room without any words of best wishes. Audrey and I sat there in that tiny room looking at each other, thinking that someone else would come in and see how we were handling the bad news. Nobody came. After 15 minutes we decided that we were finished, left, and flew home. That was five months ago. Every day we sit and look at each other and talk about dying. Now we are tired of talking and resent each other. We spent 35 years deeply in love and neither of us can bear to see it all end in bitterness."

"Doctor Jack," I said, "let me give you some advice. You are used to giving it to other people, but today I'm going to turn the tables on you. Do you and Audrey feel that all your affairs are in order? Wills? Making wrongs right? All the things two people need to do before death comes?"

"Not really," he said.

"Go home and put all things in order so that if you should die two days from now, you'd be ready. Then put that behind you. You and Audrey get up every morning and enjoy each other. Eat out. Play games. Relax by the ocean. Walk in the woods. Look into each other's eyes and say romantic things and touch each other gently. Sing together. Listen to good music. Go to concerts. Say 'I love you' in dozens of ways every day. Live each day with fresh love and passion. Life is for living. Dying will take care of itself."

I will never forget what Jack said. "Oh, Audrey, why didn't we think of this five months ago? Let's not waste any more time. Let's live the time that's left."

Audrey had tears running down her cheeks as she said, "Jack, I guess I was too scared to think of living. Yes, I want to live and make every minute count. I want to spend every day enjoying you instead of wallowing in thoughts of death."

Several times prior to Jack's death I received notes in the mail from him and Audrey telling me that they were madly in love and living every minute enjoying it. I tell you this not to minimize the phenomenon of chronic loss and long-term grief but to emphasize that this approach brought meaning to Jack's last months of life and also made Audrey's mourning much easier. Chronic illness has its lasting pain, but we can use constructive approaches that will help us not give in to despair.

I don't know much about how children grieve, because almost all the studies on grief have concentrated on adults. And the few studies on children have not involved a broad cross-section of the population.

Several years ago I attended a weekend intensive with Dr. J. William Worden at the University of Chicago and enjoyed his presentation. More recently he presented a seminar at a community college near my home in Muskegon, Michigan. He announced that he was launching a longitudinal study of children in grief after pointing out the great need for research in this area. His observations had given him a strong hunch that children grieve for a long time. From my own limited experience I have the same feeling and eagerly await the results of Dr. Worden's study.

When I served as chaplain of an eating disorders unit I was struck by the sadness on the face of a 15-year-old girl. She distrusted our staff and tried to withdraw from the other patients. One day she disappeared from the unit. Alerting the security officers in the hospital, we launched an all-out search for her.

I walked all over the expansive grounds of the hospital. After an hour of searching I headed back to my office. As I headed across the parking lot I glanced up at the tall nursing tower. There in the sixth-floor lobby I saw her thin face looking out at the hot Texas landscape. The sixth floor was closed. Nobody had thought of looking there, and nobody ever found out how she gained access to that level.

Quickly I made my way to the sixth floor. There she was, her thin body shaking underneath two sweatsuits. I put my arm around her shoulder and said, "A penny for your thoughts."

"I'm thinking that I wish my daddy would put his arm around me. I don't remember that ever happening. I guess I never was a little girl. They expected me to take care of everything around the house. I cleaned. I cooked. I settled fights. Everything. The counselor had a meeting with my parents, but they think it's a joke. They won't agree to working it out at home."

"You've lost your childhood?"

"Never had one to lose. I'd like to be a child, but I don't guess that will ever happen."

My little 15-year-old friend didn't know how to adjust to a lost childhood. She felt fearfully out of control. Nothing she did cured her family's sickness. Only one thing seemed to be in her control—her eating. She was starving herself, and her parents didn't seem to care.

Unfortunately the insurance company refused to pay for further treatment. For all practical purposes she was a little waif, sent back to a family that didn't want her. Often in times of quiet reflection my mind goes back to that little face in the sixth-floor window. I imagine she is still mourning the loss of childhood.

A frightened 7-year-old boy slid up on the big chair in my study. His legs were too short to hang down. I stared at the bottoms of his shoes. His father had died two years ago, and now he was angry at the world. He fought both with the kids on his street and those at school.

I asked him about his father. For just a few seconds Ricky talked about the death, then he went to my bookshelf and pulled out a storybook. "Will you read me a story?"

After three stories I asked him another question about his father. Just a few words came out. Then he launched into an extended lecture about science fiction and space travel. I knew I was in for a long journey with Ricky.

After months and months of sessions, he finally showed signs of his anger lifting. "Do you know what?" he said one day. "I don't fight at school anymore. When I'm ready to leave for school I tell anger, 'Anger, you get behind that door and don't come out until I get home, hear me?' Then when I go to school I don't get angry at the kids, and I don't fight. When I get home I say to anger, 'OK, now you can come out.' Then I go down the street and fight with the neighbor kids."

Although disappointed, I told myself that I had to hang in there. I knew I was in this for a long journey. Gradually I saw more signs of progress, and we terminated our regular sessions and concluded with a few follow-up sessions during the next six months.

When I moved from that city I was surprised to see a horse galloping across my front yard. Sitting high in the saddle was 12-year-old Ricky. He had come to thank me for all the help I had given him. I was proud of Ricky.

As I write this chapter I am waiting for my 15-year-old friend Julie to come. Having lost her mother and father to cancer a couple years ago, she is now staying with a relative she does not like. The rules are strict, and the house is noisy. Her privacy is gone, so she has no place in the house to think and talk and cry.

"I spend time when everyone else is asleep thinking about what I'd be like if my mother were still alive. We were friends, and she was very wise. Now I don't have any plans for my life. My future is all gone. I don't know where I'm going and what will become of me. I just go to school in the morning, and when I come home I don't talk to anyone. Then I go to bed and the next morning do it all over again. It's like I died too."

I tell her that adjusting to her parents' death will take a long time and that I have no magic cure. But what I do have is time and friendship for her. She knows that she can visit anytime she feels like it or call me on the phone when she is afraid and empty inside.

America is not very friendly to children. Abused and neglected, they often get off to a bad start because of irresponsible parents. Violence and perversion through so-called entertainment poison their minds. Disease and random killings rip parents away from them. As a result their wounds are so deep that I sometimes wonder if they can ever heal.

Then I'm reminded of the hundreds of elementary school children I've spoken to over the past 10 years. I think of their sad heart cries expressed in the presence of their fellow students. I remember the notes the children wrote to me after our sessions ended. They told me that they would be all right.

I knew they'd be all right when I remembered a note that Tammie wrote to her father shortly after her mother died of breast cancer. "Dear Daddy, I love you very much because you are the very best daddy in all the world and I want you to know that if you are ever sad and need somebody to talk to you can talk to me. After all, that's what kids are for. Love and kisses, Tammie."

Please be there for children who hurt. Be there for a long time.

I have lectured in hundreds of cities to clergy and conducted seminars for dozens of churches. In almost every situation I have heard the cry of chronic grief from the lips of parents who have lost their children from the church. I understood their pain from personal experience.

My oldest brother left the church of his childhood. Although much younger than he, I vividly recall his frequent visits to our home. He ridiculed my parents for being duped by "that crazy religion" and took great delight in swearing and using vulgar terms in their presence. I watched my parents' faces turn sad. My heart ached for them, but there wasn't a thing I could do. Their grief and heartache were constant. I know because I heard them talking together about it many times.

A kind friend of mine watched his son walk away from God. The boy went to the most wicked part of the big city and threw his life away. When he was drunk or penniless he would call home. His parents bailed him out of jail, gave him shelter, and bought him new clothes. They found him jobs and provided medical treatment for him. Still he turned his back on God and them. When they begged their son to go back to church, he spurned their pleas. Finally they refused to have anything more to do with him.

One day as I talked to the father I suggested that the son he dreamed of having was lost to him and would never return. Even if he did come back to God and the church, he would not be the same son. His whole experience would leave its mark. He would be a different person.

"Why don't you say goodbye to the son you hoped to have? Say farewell to him. Then you will be able to say hello to the son you do have. You will be able to say hello to him as he is, for what he is, and thus free him to become more than he is."

That was a new thought to the father, but he promised to consider it carefully. Months later he shared with me that his son was visiting the home again. They had lifted the ban. Furthermore, he was expressing regret for having thrown his life away. The father and mother simply let the son know that they loved him just the same. No longer pushing and cajoling him, they just accepted him. That acceptance promised to be an opening of a hard heart and the closing of chronic mourning for two parents.

Chapter Thirteen

Dying Solitaire

In my 14 years of walking into sickrooms I've seen hundreds of patients playing solitaire. I've always viewed it as rather lonely and futile, because the person has no interaction with another person who understands card playing.

At the same time I've met too many patients dying solitaire. Solitaire because family and friends were not there to interact, to listen, to weep, to laugh, to hold, to care. For these patients mourning lingered on and on until unconsciousness mercifully ended the solitaire. No human being should have to spend the last months or years of life in this way.

Abraham was in a private room. During his three-week stay not a soul came to visit him. Because all the nurses had noticed this fact, they asked me if I would spend some time with him. They had so many patients that the luxury of sitting down and visiting with him was out of the question.

The man was dying. The doctors told him that just as soon as his wounds healed he was to go home and put things in order. Now he was spending his last days in the hospital.

"Tell me, Abraham, about your family," I invited.

"Family? Can't say as I have family. Well, I have a common-law wife that lived with me once in a while, but she hasn't been around in a long, long time. Have a sister. She heard somehow that I was awful sick. Came by asking for the house, but I told her she was never around when I was well, and I wasn't about to give her the house. So that's the way it is. Can't say as I have family."

"What was it like growing up?" I asked.

"Funny you should ask. I was thinking of that the other night. My folks were drunk all the time, so I left home when I was 9. Went to stay with an uncle in Chicago. He was a bad drinker and would whip me for no reason. I stayed till I was 11. Then I was a street urchin for a long time. A few folk took pity on me and offered me shelter and food for a spell, but I pretty much fended for myself. Then when I was old enough to work I came here and took a job in the cereal factory. Bought me a little place on the north side and saved a little money and a few company stocks. And that's all I have to my name."

"And now the doctor tells you you're dying. Who do you have to be with you?"

"Not a soul, sir. Not a soul."

As Abraham spoke, the tears flowed freely. Because a surgical procedure made it impossible for him to swallow, he asked me every few minutes for a spoonful of chipped ice that he let melt in his mouth. I held the emesis basin to his mouth so he could spit out the water. Then I emptied the glass of ice chips and the emesis basin.

"Before I leave you, Abraham, is there anything I can do for you?"

"Yes sir. You can read the shepherd's psalm."

" 'The Lord is my Shepherd; I shall not want . . .' " As I read, he stared up toward the ceiling. His big brown eyes filled with tears again. His pockmarked chin quivered, and his big bony hand reached down and held my right hand resting on the bed.

" 'Surely goodness and mercy shall follow me all the days of my life: and I will dwell in the house of the Lord for ever.' "

Quiet filled the room. Abraham closed his eyes and squeezed my hand tightly.

"There surely must be more I can do for you, Abraham," I urged.

"Yes sir. You can give me a glass of ice chips. A big glass."

I went to the nursing station and filled a large styrofoam cup with ice chips. Then I pulled a chair up to his bed and slowly fed him ice chips and caught the water in the emesis basin. All was quiet as he finished the entire cupful of ice.

"Mr. Chaplain, what time is it now?"

"Three-fifteen."

"Mr. Chaplain, you've spent 45 minutes with me. I can't tell you how much I appreciate it. I can't believe you've spent 45 minutes with me."

I have often thought of him and tried to imagine what it must be like to mourn the loss of your own life all alone. It is a long road that doesn't end until death.

I'll never forget what he told me during one of our last visits. We were chatting about how frightening it must have been for him when he was a street urchin in Chicago. He looked at me with those deep brown eyes and said, "Life has its bitter and its sweet. I haven't had any sweet yet, but maybe that's what death is all about."

A young woman in Ohio was bedridden with cancer of the bone. Her husband isolated her in a back bedroom and would not let any visitors enter. I was an intern pastor at the time. The husband refused my request to see his wife until only two weeks before her death. To my horror, I learned that he seldom entered her room himself. She had endured years of illness in seclusion—seclusion that must have seemed like eternity.

I held her fragile hand in mine as I greeted her and told her my name. Then I sat down next to her bed, speechless in the face of what I saw. Finally I gained my composure enough to speak.

"I don't have the faintest idea of what you have gone through. I don't even know what to say. I'm a minister of the gospel, but I didn't come here to preach at you. I simply want to know if there is anything I can do to make this easier for you."

"I'm happy you were able to come today. There isn't anything anyone can do for me physically. Many bones in my body have broken just lying here in bed. The cancer will take my life. You can help me by telling me how I can be ready to meet God. I don't know anything about it. You'll have to make it simple. I'll try to understand."

"God wants more than anything else to have you in heaven with Him. He is so eager to have you there that He sent His Son, Jesus, to die for you. His death on the cross provided the gift of eternal life. Today He extends that free gift to you. All you need to do is tell God that you are accepting that gift. Tell Him you are sorry for disappointing Him in your life. Tell Him you are accepting the gift of life in heaven with Him. Then thank Him for the wonderful gift and keep thanking Him for life in heaven every day you awaken."

"That sounds easy enough to me, but I don't know how to talk to God. Can you help me?"

I prayed a simple prayer of acceptance, and she repeated it after me. Then thanking me, she closed her eyes and went to sleep while I quietly left the room.

Two days before she died I went to the hospital where she had been admitted. She lay in a private room at the far end of a large ward. A tent had been situated over the bed to keep the weight of the covers off of her emaciated body. Not a person was in the room. Her family had not been there all day.

When I greeted her she turned her face toward me, fear written all over it. With her thin hands she reached for my hands, but her grip was unbelievably strong. I could not release my hands. Extreme weakness left her unable to speak. Quietly I quoted promises from Scripture, told her how thrilling it will be when the two of us can visit together in heaven, and prayed to God on her behalf. Her grip loosened, and she fell asleep.

I was the last person to visit her before she slipped into a coma. She was forced to face the loss of her own life alone. Also she found herself forced to say goodbye in solitude to every relationship she ever had, every hope and dream she had ever dreamed. And I do not believe that she was able to accomplish that alone. I still think she was troubled in mind and despairingly lonely during the course of her illness.

Chronic grief in the lives of people with a life-threatening disease is more apt to happen when they lack satisfying relationships. When family cohesiveness vanishes, the ill person is more likely to be despondent, to desire death, to contemplate suicide, and to experience depression. On the other hand, an ill person survives longer and lives meaningfully and purposefully when family and surroundings are pleasant.

Mario owned a large Texas ranch. By managing it carefully, he made a decent living on that harsh land. Then cancer struck. Now Mario was confined to his motorized lounge chair.

His wife placed his chair in the middle of the living room where he could oversee all the kitchen activities and look out the windows at his ranch. From his window he could view the cattle sheds and watch the hired hands doing the chores. She let Mario know that he was the boss. Good at giving orders, he loved every minute of it.

I visited Mario when the apricots were just beginning to ripen. He instructed me to look after those apricots and make sure they didn't get overripe. I'd walk out to the orchard, check on the apricots, and let him know how they were coming along. My son and I sat and listened to Mario tell about his move from New Jersey to Texas. He chronicled every event that led from poverty to the ownership of his ranch. His stories captivated us, and Mario was happy to be socially in command.

His family treated him like a king. They showered him with hugs and kisses. A few relatives from New Jersey came and spent a week or two, helped around the ranch, and chatted about old times in New Jersey. A happy man, Mario lived far longer than our expectations.

Mario was gone by the time the apricots finished ripening. I went out to the ranch and picked the last of them. It saddened me that I couldn't report to the boss, but I was happy that he had really lived the last year of his life.

After watching scores of families relating to their very sick loved ones, I am convinced that isolation and depersonalization happen because of misunderstandings about people who are facing life-threatening illness. When I hear comments like "Mother is dying of cancer," I prefer to say "Mother is living with cancer." I believe sick people are alive and interested in life. That's the way they want to be treated.

I assisted in the development of two hospices and volunteered my services to several others. It was my privilege to go into the homes of scores of ill people and talk about life. In turn I listened to them tell me about life. We took hundreds of journeys from our armchairs to places both exotic and mundane. As a natural part of their deep conversations about life, they shared their concerns about death. Together we worked through the death-related issues. They accomplished their grieving and went about their living in spite of the disease.

A nurse stopped me one day in the hall. "Larry, can you stop in to see Maude in 312? She's dying, and I don't know how to talk to her. I don't know what to say."

"What part of the country do you come from, Maude?" I began.

"The beautiful state of Maine," she responded proudly.

"Ah-h-h, Maine. You picked blueberries and milked cows. Right?"

"Of course. Many years while growing up. I love blueberries and milking the old cow outside on a cool morning. Those were wonderful days. Never forget them," she said enthusiastically.

"My sisters and I milked cows ever since we were old enough to tuck our heads in the cow's side just in front of the hind leg. Daddy told us that way we could feel the cow wanting to kick so we could be prepared for it. It didn't work. A cow named Bones sent me flying one morning." She chuckled about her misfortune.

"We hobbled the kickers," she added. "Didn't take any chances. It was a good life up there in Maine. I miss it. Talking about it makes it all come back so clear."

"What brought a good New Englander like you to Michigan?"

"I married a man from Michigan, and I followed my man."

For days we swapped stories about farming and picking blueberries. She had a special look of childhood joy in her eyes when she told her tales. We laughed together until the tears came. Then one day out of the blue she said, "You know I'm dying, don't you?"

"Who told you that?"

"The doctor. That's what he told me."

"Well, are you ready to die?" I asked.

"I'm on good terms with God, if that's what you mean."

"That's part of it. How about your will?"

"That's been made out for years. I don't have any enemies that I know of."

"How about funeral arrangements?"

"Now that's one thing I haven't done yet. Maybe you could help me with that."

For the next half hour we wrote down her wishes. Funeral home, preacher, songs, method of burial. She handled the whole thing very matter-of-factly. Then she told me another funny story about her childhood in Maine.

Hours before Maude died I walked into her room. She was very weak, but she sat up in her bed and, leaning against the railing, stared intently at me. "What are you looking for, Maude?"

"I just wanted to make sure it was you," she said. Then she lay back on her pillow and began to reminisce about picking blueberries in old Maine.

Maude confirmed in my mind that ill people feel free to do their grieving and do it well when someone is willing to treat them as alive. But I have met people with a life-threatening illness who have not grieved well because the people in their life refuse to talk about it. I've heard it called the "horse on the table syndrome." People come to a fancy dinner. Standing on the table is a big horse. All the guests see the horse. The host sees the horse. Everyone knows it is a horse on the table, but not a single person talks about it. A life-threatening illness is often the horse on the table. The whole family and the ill person know the disease is there, but nobody will talk about it. As a result, active grieving doesn't occur. Unfinished business goes uncared-for, wishes are not expressed, and expressions of affection go unsaid.

Some of the hospice patients I have met died socially and emotionally long before they died physically. The medical people in contact with them focused almost solely on the disease and treatment. This has always seemed to me a good way to shorten a person's life and make it very dismal.

Once I visited a woman who had been focusing exclusively on her medical condition. Her daughter complained that her mother sat in a living room chair all day and vowed she could not walk without assistance. Deciding to attempt to change her focus, I thought my mountain dulcimer would be a sure way to do the job.

"Dory, you and I are going to have a good old hoedown. Just let me get this dulcimer tuned up here, and you and I are going to sing." Striking up the chord, I began "You Are My Sunshine" and kept a close eye on her. Sure enough, she was tapping her foot in time to the music. On the second verse she rose from her chair, walked to the opposite side of the room, picked up a cloth bag, and returned to her chair. From the bag she pulled a musical saw and a bow that she ran over a rosin block. In moments the whine of her saw blended with the soft sounds of my dulcimer. We played and sang for a good half hour. Laughter filled the room, and her medical focus shattered.

On my way out the door Dory's daughter said, "I can't believe my eyes. My mom actually walked unassisted. I can't believe it."

A red-cheeked old Texan was a patient in the oncology unit. As he sank into depression, his appetite disappeared, his face became gray, and the light in his eyes grew dimmer by the day. Then I discovered that he was the grand champion of the Old Fiddlers' Contest held in Alvarado every summer. "Somebody told me you play a fiddle," I told him.

"I played fiddle some in my day."

"I don't believe it. Who ever heard of a fiddler without a fiddle? I won't believe it till I hear it with my own ears."

"Well, look here. You can't bring a fiddle to a hospital."

"Who says you can't? It's your room. You're paying big money for it."

"You suppose I'd be allowed?"

"Of course. Tell your family to bring it in here. If there are complaints, just send them to me."

That night the oncology unit had a face-lift. The old fiddler had the twinkle in his eyes, and his cheeks were rosy again. Other patients perked up. Some walked down the hall to listen. Nurses and technicians came to his room.

"Did you recognize that one? That was the 'Irish Washer Woman.' Now what'll the next one be?"

The ice was broken. In the coming days the old fiddler came out of his shell. He talked about his illness and shared his feelings with the hospital personnel. As he came to terms with his physical condition, he also realized that he was still alive and able to make other lives brighter.

Adjusting to a loss, whether it is the death of a friend or a threat to your personal life, takes a lot of energy. For that reason it is important to maintain as much balance as possible in the day-to-day program. Like the wise man said, there is a time to laugh, a time to cry, a time to gather, and a time to scatter. There is a time for solitude and a time to be gregarious. There is a time to look death right in the face. And there is a time to turn away from it.

Mourning characterizes the entire journey from diagnosis to death. It is much easier when it is not done solitaire fashion.

Chapter Fourteen

Caregiver Mourning

The director of the neonatal intensive-care unit in a neighboring hospital asked me to visit her. Tension between staff members, increased sick days off, and a rise in staff turnover were threatening to render the unit ineffective in its high-risk work with newborns.

The unit discharged a girl after she had spent the first three years of her life in the unit. Two nurses began arguing over which of them the little girl considered her "mother." A physician was becoming more tense around the staff. Head nurses began complaining about the high stress of the job. Something had to be done.

The director and I developed a support program that included a regularly scheduled meeting designed for clearing the emotional air, a periodic meeting to plan the care for a high-risk infant, an emergency group called at any time by a staff member feeling high stress levels, and an impromptu meeting between an individual staff member and a hospital social worker.

A month after the support program started, positive changes began to take place. I received a letter from the director stating that turnover of staff had slowed and the emotional tone in the unit was much healthier.

This experience taught me that mourning is a constant component of caregiving. Just as mourning patients and families need support to mourn, so caregivers also need a support system if they are going to do effective caregiving very long.

I know nurses who work in oncology units and lose one patient after another. They become attached to patients. A favorite person dies. Before they have a chance to mourn, another patient succumbs. The backlog of grief mounts, until they become numb. If such special people receive no help, they either leave their profession or change to a different type of nursing.

A large Catholic hospital asked me to help train the nursing staff of a new oncology unit. During the first eight months of the unit's operation the affiliated physicians admitted their sickest patients. In that time 11 of them died.

Nurses began threatening to leave the unit. In an effort to prevent this, I assisted in the development of a support group. For the next six months the hospital called me to attend the nurses who were losing a patient. I sat by the bed with nurse and family. The nurse and I remained in the room after the death and helped the family begin the process of grieving. Then after the family left I gathered the nurses together, and we all talked, laughed, and cried together. We affirmed the caregiver for a job well done.

Without this type of support, caregivers develop a professional aloofness that cheats the patients and family of good care and also reduces job satisfaction. Without such support, caregivers know that they cannot survive the continual loss and grief. They develop a shield to hide behind so they can cope with the emotional pressure. But that becomes a barrier to many other things.

I have seen nurses enter a room and be attentive to an IV pump, yet never pay attention to the moaning patient in the bed. And I have seen clergy enter the sickroom, utter a fast Scripture reading and prayer, and exit the room without inquiring about the spiritual needs of the sick parishioner. I've seen hospital housekeepers swishing a mop and softly whistling in the room of a terminally ill patient without once looking at the patient. None of these special people deserve criticism if we expect them to care without being cared for. Working around loss day after day takes an emotional toll on caregivers.

Many authors have written about the emotional demands of caring for the ill, the dying, and the bereaved. Research projects and general articles frequently appear in professional journals. In 1984 Therese A. Rando advised caregivers to grieve for those they lose. She reiterated her advice in her more recent volume, *Treatment of Complicated Mourning* (Champaign, Ill.: Research Press, 1993).

In the 14 years I have worked as a chaplain in hospitals and in the 18 years I have conducted bereavement support groups, I have discovered a few approaches to adjusting to the types of losses that buffet caregivers day after day.

1. Resolve your own personal grief as soon as possible. Be aware that you will experience subsequent temporary upsurges of grief for months after the loss occurs. When this happens, arrange to lighten your caregiving load until you have adjusted to the new or renewed implication of your loss.

An oncology nurse lost her 2-year-old granddaughter in a car accident. Returning to work a few days after the funeral, she thought she could sail through her work without her loss hindering her. At home she removed all the pictures of her granddaughter from the walls and shelves and put all the child's toys in a spare room and closed the door. No reminders, no pain—or so she thought.

Eight months after the funeral she entertained another grandchild in her home. She gave that child a few of the toys that she had closed away in the spare room. The next day she went to the oncology unit and watched a favorite patient die. When a second patient experienced a cardiac arrest and had to be resuscitated, she fell apart and informed her supervisor that she could not continue her shift. The supervisor reprimanded her for not being over her grief. This made matters worse, and the nurse walked off the job. The next day the hospital gave her a leave of absence and placed her on probation for six months.

Two years after my son died I began working in a very busy emergency room. One day the ambulance brought a young man into the emergency room, dead on arrival. The family arrived and I tried to minister to them, but I knew I was personalizing their pain. I knew I was not being helpful to them. The young man in the treatment room could have been my son as far as my emotions were concerned. When the family left the hospital I walked out into the hot Texas air with tears streaming down my face, saying to myself, "I don't understand why this is happening. Why, God? Why?"

Knowing that I had not adequately grieved for my own son, I did my best to face the pain. A few months later a major accident occurred on the freeway, bringing a young man the same age as Jeff to the emergency room. As I attended the family this time, I was able to differentiate my loss and pain from that of theirs. Thus I was able to focus on the needs of the family. When they left the hospital I walked back to my office, thanking God all the way that He had helped me take a giant step forward.

2. Do not get caught up in the fine details of the other person's pain. Listen carefully in an effort to see the whole picture. Look for the profile of disequilibrium and develop options for planting that person's feet on the path to restored equilibrium.

One cannot be aloof, however. To make a good diagnosis and think of workable options requires active listening. You will occasionally need to ask questions and request clarification of certain issues. That way the grieving person will know that you are really tuned in to his or her feelings.

3. Make sure your life is well-balanced. Only a well-balanced person can stand up to the stresses of working with grieving people. Good nutrition, adequate rest, sufficient exercise, plenty of water, recreation, time for relaxation, time for creative solitude, and a steady relationship with God are some of the components of balance.

Stress management is more than developing coping skills. It is carefully analyzing every area of your life. If you are putting a lot of energy into one area and gaining little or no rewards from that investment, it is time either to change the area, to change your attitude about that area, or to exit that area. We do have the ability to decide when we are expending more energy than we should. Each of us can say no. Being temperate in all things includes the demands we allow others and ourselves to place upon us.

4. Have enough close relationships outside the workplace to provide adequate dialogue. Dialogue is the elixir of life—the sharing of hopes, dreams, joys, and sorrows with a confidant. It is a relationship or relationships in which you give and receive affirmation, appreciation, praise, and a sense of connectedness. Adequate dialogue outside the workplace prevents the caregiver from relying on patients to meet basic human needs.

5. Grieve the losses of patients as they happen. Share your feelings with the patient.

A cancer patient was hoping for a good report from a test since the physicians had told her that the cancer could metastasize to the brain. The test revealed what she feared the most.

After her doctor shared the news with her, the entire staff felt sad. I went into her room and said, "Ann, I heard about the test. You must be very disappointed."

"I prayed and prayed because I want to live. My poor husband is like a lost puppy. He comes into this room and looks out the window. He doesn't know what to say. We just cry together. And now I don't know how he'll take this."

"Ann, you need to know that I am sad about the test. I was hoping and praying with you. And the staff on this unit are sad this morning. They told me so. But you also need to know that we are all going to work together to make this as easy as we can for you. When your husband comes this afternoon, we are going to give you time alone, but we are also going to spend some time with him. We'll help him talk it out. We'll be sad together, but we'll face it together."

By grieving with this patient, I did not have to carry the grief home with me.

6. Do not assume that you can carry the pain of others all by yourself.

My first few months working in psychiatric wards nearly overwhelmed me. I spent time with many patients and helped them examine their options in recovery. Sometimes I'd work overtime and see some patients twice a day. Then I realized that I was trying to carry the world on my shoulders. One day I walked out the back door of the hospital and looked up at the sky. "God, I've carried these people on my heart today. Now I'm going home. Please carry them the rest of the day. Please help me to understand that other staff members can care for their needs just as well as I can." That was a great breakthrough prayer that enabled me to remain healthy during my seven years in those wards.

7. Vary your work.

After a counseling session with a person in deep grief, turn to something lighter. If you have just had two deaths on a nursing unit, ask for a lighter load for a day or two.

I can remember days when I went to three and four emergencies in one morning. But those were also the days when I would make my way to the pediatrics floor to make paper airplanes with the children. It may be an unusual sight to see a chaplain and a child playing air force in the hallway, but it was a healthy activity to me, and hopefully to the child.

8. Talk openly with patients about their condition.

I have found that patients, grieving family, and other persons in crisis want to talk about their feelings. When I try to avoid such conversations, it is stressful to me, and I tend to keep a whole mountain of feelings inside.

Instead I let people know that they may have painful and perplexing feelings about their situation. I assure them that they can share those feelings with me and I won't run away. Often this opens the way for them to bring up painful topics. We have open and frank discussions and are both better off for having done so.

I believe in saying things to hurting people that I feel compelled to say. And I believe in doing things for them when I feel inclined to do them.

One day I was walking out the door of the hospital when I had an urge to tell an old woman that I loved her. She was one of those people who looked out for everyone even though she was the person with a life-threatening disease. Instantly I went back to her room.

"Alma, I had to come back and see you before going home. I want you to know how much I appreciate what you do for me when I visit you."

"Is that all you came back for?"

"No. I really came back to tell you that I love you."

"Oh, thank you! That makes all the difference in the world!"

When Alma died two days later I had no regrets, and I grieved well.

9. Take plenty of time off to recharge your emotional batteries.

I ride my racing bicycle down a 22-mile trail. In my backpack I have lunch and good books to read. Midway on the trip I relax at a picnic table with lunch and a favorite author. Sometimes I take my stunt kite to the shore of Lake Michigan, just four miles from my home. There I tug on the double lines, executing figure eights and fancy loops. I dive that vinyl bird and skim it along the water and sand. Little children stop to admire it. Other kite enthusiasts stop to engage in kite talk. Sometimes I lie down behind a sand dune and watch the wind playing games with my hot-pink kite. Sea gulls soar past and flirt with the colorful newcomer to the skies.

After a smooth landing on the singing sands of Muskegon I fold up my kite, walk back to my car, and drive along the lakeshore. My mood has soared, just as my kite was lifted up by the prevailing winds. I can face another day, another week of mourning.

Chapter Fifteen

The Exercise of Courage

Lydia and Leonard, her merchant husband, lived in a sprawling home by a lake. She never had to get her hands dirty. The groundskeeper tidied the waterfront, mowed the lawns, and kept flowers blooming from spring to autumn. Several hired domestics did the housework, so she spent her days playing bridge and throwing parties in the huge oak-paneled dining room. In her spare time she went shopping with the wives of her husband's business friends. She had no worries about running out of money.

Leonard and a close friend bought and sold properties in the city. His assets mushroomed, but he was addicted to work. Long hours and poor diet took their toll. Illness struck quickly, and Lydia became a widow before she had time to assimilate the slightest thought of his death.

A year after he died she came to a support group I was conducting. Spotting an older man in the group, she clung to him during the entire program. She appeared desperate for someone to lean on, and insisted on having a seat next to Fred. Self-distrust and indecisiveness almost paralyzed her.

By the end of five weeks I knew I had to help Lydia pull herself together. She insisted that I come to her home for personal counseling. Since she was more than three decades my senior, I had no qualms about her plan.

Meeting me at the door with a strong embrace, she declared, "Oh, it feels so good to have the strong arms of a man around me! The security I feel with a man in the house is simply unexplainable! You've had a busy morning. Now, come on into the small dining room. I've been waiting for the chance to do this."

Her *small* dining room made two of mine. On a solid oak table big enough for just two people were two china dishes and two dainty teacups. The silverware appeared new, and the tablecloth and napkins matched elegantly.

"Leonard and I always had tea several times a week. I brewed his favorite tea and baked the old family recipe tea cake he raved about so. You'll love it. You say grace, and then we can enjoy this time together."

After tea Lydia led me to the family room. There she pointed to an old clock hanging motionless on the wall. "I always depended on Leonard to keep it going," she said. "What can you do to bring it to life?"

I wound it, set the hands, and gave the pendulum a push. It ticked for 30 seconds and stopped. Repeated attempts were in vain. Obviously I did not have Leonard's touch.

Lydia then led me to the kitchen and invited me to sit down for a long chat. Suddenly I had a hunch that I was now Leonard, not Larry. My hunch was confirmed later that afternoon when she ordered me to wear old clothes on my next visit so I could pick the blackberries in Leonard's patch.

Propping my elbows on the kitchen table, I looked her in the eyes and said, "Lydia, I know what I'm about to say will sound strange. You need to ask God for courage to begin grieving for Leonard's death."

"You don't think I've done it?"

"No, I don't think you have decided to grieve actively."

She thought a moment. "I'm an old woman. I should know how to go about adjusting to my loss, but I guess I'm at my wits end. I've never had to decide about anything. Leonard made all the decisions and took care of me. I have to admit that I feel like a lost soul. How do I go about it?"

"Decide to set aside an hour each day to reconstruct and reexperience every aspect of your relationship with him. Fully experience any emotions this reminiscing might bring up. Allow the pain to happen. Before you leave that hour, write your feelings in a journal. Then write a short farewell to that particular aspect of the relationship. Say goodbye to what was but can no longer be. Leonard is not coming back, Lydia. You need to ask God for the courage to believe that and to say farewell."

To my surprise, she agreed that her world was indeed shattered and gone. Then she made the decision to look at her life realistically and to begin openly and actively grieving.

In the months following that first visit Lydia and I ate a lot of tea cake and drank a lot of tea, but it was as Larry, not Leonard. I helped her with her toughest farewells. Eventually she roamed her large home with me, relating memories in a relaxed mood.

One afternoon she and I took a stroll down to the lake where she talked about rising tax rates for lakefront properties, worries about hiring reliable help, and the fear of rattling around in a big house one more winter.

"A few months ago I told you to ask God for courage to begin grieving," I said. "Now I think it's time to ask for courage to stop grieving. No more books about grief. No more support groups. No more deliberate rehearsal of the relationship. Now it's time to decide that you will close that chapter and begin a new one. There will be some subsequent upsurges of grief along the way, but you'll handle those when they come. Now it's time to plan the next chapter of your life."

We both looked up at her large home on the knoll overlooking the lake. She quietly reflected on the good times with family in the house.

"You're right, Larry. This is too much for me. I'll sell it to my son. He has asked to have it. I'll not spend another winter here. A new retirement village just opened west of here. I'll look into it. I think I could be very happy there."

Reading Lydia's story makes it sound so easy, but the exercise of courage took her through many frightening places. The essential thought I want to emphasize is that she decided to begin active grieving. This enabled her to decide to stop active grief and to construct a new life for herself.

Learning to live on a different income, in a different environment, with different people, and with new goals takes courage.

Della exercised that courage. She decided to weep and to stay in the same house her husband had built. It was no longer their house, but hers. The large living room remains closed except when company comes. She lives in her large kitchen. Next to the windows with a southernly exposure she has a single bed, her favorite rocker, and her books, tape player, and dozens of other items she frequently needs.

She manages her rental homes with skill. Self-reliance and tough-minded business savvy have combined to earn a living for her for the rest of her life.

When Della needs people, she knows how to achieve togetherness. She decided to volunteer time to help others. Boredom never sets in, because she has goals that reach far beyond her life expectancy.

Courage is indispensable if you are going to really live after your loss. But acquiring such courage is not an innate human ability. I'm convinced that it is a gift from God.

A psychologist friend attended my son's funeral. He asked me, "Now what do you have to say to secular psychologists who maintain that faith doesn't make a difference in how we adjust to loss?"

"They need to go back and do better research," came my immediate response.

Still of the same opinion, I can truthfully say that I was afraid to begin grieving. I had helped other people get through losses, but when it was my heart that was breaking, I had to struggle with the urge to run away from grief. So I asked God for the courage to face the pain with my head held high.

Reorganizing my life produced contradictory emotions. I wanted my equilibrium restored, but equating this with disloyalty and desertion sent me into a mental tailspin. Structuring my present and looking ahead to the future required courage that I simply didn't have. So I asked God for an extra dose.

My friend Art was in the last stages of MS. His remarkable peace of mind impressed me. "I watch you every day. I listen to your words. I come to visit you and lift you up, but you are usually the one who does the lifting. I guess I don't understand."

"It's simple, Chaplain. It's God and I. God and I. That's it. What more can I say?"

Art told me that he had struggled with the MS when it was first diagnosed, but he had finally admitted that he was powerless to handle the loss. That's when he was able to grasp the strength and courage that God offers. In his weakness God's strength alone could accomplish its task.

Dick was recovering from lung cancer surgery. The doctor had told him the survival rate was not a pretty picture, but even that depended a lot on his attitude. He thought that over for a long time. Ever since the diagnosis Dick had felt as if he were the only cancer victim in the whole world. His courage plummeted, and he became a recluse.

When he thumbed through his Bible one day he began to pray aloud with his eyes wide open. "God, what I need is courage to make the rest of my time count." Then he stumbled onto a book about an organization started by Orville Kelly called Make Today Count. That rang some bells for Dick. Reminding himself that there must be other people in his city who had cancer, he talked to his doctor about it. The doctor's secretary contacted other cancer patients for their permission to let Dick get into contact with them. That was the beginning of what he called "real living."

First he had to raise money to start his support group. One friend donated scraps of copper tubing, another donated plexiglass, still another donated small chain material, and a fishing buddy threw in a few spools of fishing line. Dick was ready to go into business. He sold dozens of wind chimes for $20 each. The money established the support group. Not only did I hear wind chime music at my home every day, I also had the privilege of being the chaplain for Dick's "Make Today Count" organization.

We had a big cake and lemonade the night we celebrated Dick's seventh year after lung cancer surgery. Dick told the group that he had to credit God for the courage and the strength to face a life-threatening disease. He promised all of us that whatever time he had left he would give to us and to any other cancer patients who cared to join the group. That's been more than 10 years ago. I don't know what has happened in Dick's life since, but I am still celebrating his courage.

Unresolved grief has the power to stop a person from functioning. To go on with life requires the bold request for courage and the tough decision to do things you would not ordinarily do.

Marvin worked in a profession that handled people problems.

His work was extremely demanding and stressful. Distractions and personal problems could spell disaster for the recipients of his services. That's why the death of his young wife led to his taking a leave of absence.

Although he had decided to grieve actively, reexperiencing their relationship was very difficult to do. Grief kept him from bringing to mind the details of their relationship. I asked him where he and his wife had lived most of their married life, and suggested that he return to that city and walk through the two homes they had dwelt in.

He asked me to pray that he'd have the courage to make the trip and knock on the doors of those two special houses. I assured him that our prayers for courage would be answered. Marvin took the two-day trip by car so he would have plenty of time to think, pray, and cry.

At the last minute he decided to take his 9-year-old son along. It probably was a factor in his gaining easy access to the houses. The current owners were very understanding and pleased to be a part of his journey toward adjustment.

Marvin and his son slowly went from room to room, talking about special events and family fun. A walk in the backyards was part of the process. After each house visit they climbed into the car, found a quiet spot to park, and cried together.

While they were still in the area they decided to take one more difficult step toward their adjustment. They visited some of the places they had taken family vacations. The swimming holes, mountain trails, and scenic overlooks flooded their minds with good memories.

Their trip home they spent reminiscing about the pieces of life they had lived in their former home. On the second day of the return trip Marvin did a lot of talking to himself and to God.

"God, You gave me the courage to do the most difficult thing I've ever done since my wife died. I've done my part. Now it's Your turn. I need a peace inside me that will enable me to write the next chapter of my life. I was able to go back and walk the trails of earlier years, but I can't manufacture peace. That's Your department."

Late in the evening the boy was asleep on the back seat. Marvin had been listening to quiet music on a station located in the large city he now called home. Just as the night skyline came into view Marvin sensed that peace had come. He was able to make a decision to stop grieving and start building plans for his future.

If you went to that big city to see Marvin, you'd not find him. He took a job in the area in which he and his wife had spent their happy years together. Occasionally I hear from him. He reports that he is grateful to God for giving him the courage to close a door on his grief and open a door to life again.

The exercise of courage, like the exercise of the body, is easy to put off. It seems to be more comfortable remaining in the confusion of grief. I know that sounds strange, but I have met scores of people who refuse to take the courageous step onto the next page of life. If they could only understand that God has more than enough courage and strength to get them through the confusion to a new life on the other side.

I have always appreciated the experience of the apostle Paul. Struggling with some almost overwhelming problem, perhaps a painful physical ailment, he begged God to heal him because he did not think he could cope with it much longer. God's response was, "My grace is all you need, for my power is strongest when you are weak" (2 Cor. 12:9, TEV).

One of my college professors defined grace as God's power and courage that enables you to do what you can't do alone. I've done my share of hesitating to grieve. I would not criticize those who hold back, but I would recommend that they think about the definition of grace shared with me by my teacher. If you decide to start grieving and ultimately to stop grieving, you will agree with me that the courage is there.

I grew up on a Pennsylvania farm on which every member of the family was expected to work. When haying time came my father assigned me the task of pulling in the end of the big bull rope after the tractor pulled it far beyond the barn. The other end of the rope was attached to a large fork that lifted the hay into the mow. The tractor pulled the load up in the air. Someone had to retrieve the rope by hand to prepare for another load.

The first time I retrieved it I was afraid I couldn't pull the weight of that bulky rope. But I wasn't about to let my sisters think I wasn't up to the task. Grabbing that rope, I yanked with all my might. It was surprisingly light. As I drew the last few feet of the rope into the barn

I glanced over my shoulder. There was my father pulling on the rope behind me.

When I thought about the long journey of mourning ahead of me after my son's death I remembered my father's big strong arms tugging on that rope. I wanted very much to believe that God would be pulling with me. Looking back, I am convinced that I did not handle the weight of my grief by myself for one single day.

Recently I thumbed through the book of Hebrews in the New Testament and came across "For God has said, 'I will never leave you; I will never abandon you.' Let us be bold, then, and say, 'The Lord is my helper, I will not be afraid. What can anyone do to me?'" (Heb. 13:5, 6, TEV).

A little investigation revealed that the word "bold" is derived from the same word rendered "courage." To me that means that I can be right up front about asking God for the courage I need to face my situations. I can tackle my loss with a generous amount of assertiveness. If God gives me boldness and courage, He means for me to use it. (I imagine a good theologian could tear my interpretation to shreds, but that's what came to me as I pondered that Scripture passage.)

I'm certainly not going to tell you that you need exercise courage and boldness only once and then you miraculously have your balance to go prancing through the rest of your life. The exercise of courage is a process that takes you over many mountains and through many canyons. With each exercise you gain strength to live life a little more fully than you did the day before.

I learned about this from Jenny, an 82-year-old patient. The nurses told me that her husband had just died in a nursing home, but Jenny was too sick to attend the funeral. They were concerned for her emotional health. I stopped by her room to see what I could do to help.

"Jenny, your good nurses are concerned about you. They told me that your husband died this morning at the nursing home. How are you going to go through this painful experience?"

"Chaplain, don't you worry your head about the likes of me. Don't you see I'm an old lady? This business of losing a dear one is nothing new to me. I've been over the way many a mile. This ain't the first time my heart's ached. I lost five children in my days. Each one that passed on was a heartache. I cried and I shouted and I talked and I prayed to the good Lord for strength. Each time I picked up and went on about my business. That wasn't Jenny doing that. That was the doings of the Lord. And I plan to do the same with my husband. When I get out of this hospital I'll do lots of crying, talking, screaming, and praying to the good Lord. And He'll help me just like He did all the other times."

"Jenny, I wish I had your courage and your faith so that when I go through heartache I can go on like you have."

"Don't go saying you want Jenny's courage and faith. Jenny has nothing to do with it. It all has to do with the good Lord. It is His courage and faith, not Jenny's. Now you just go on and tell them nurses not to worry about Jenny. She'll be doing just fine, you wait and see."

Her exercise of courage still influences my life. At the time I visited with her I thought she had a rather childlike way of looking at things, but then I remembered that Jesus suggested that we all need that simple, elemental way of taking life as it comes.

I'm still on the long journey of mourning, but I think I am learning to take the curves and the potholes with a little more grace, thanks to Jenny and all the other fellow travelers I have been privileged to know.

I highly recommend the exercise of courage!

Epilogue

My son Jeff struggled long over what his major would be in college. Rather than choose between theology and English, he earned both majors. And he skillfully blended both majors in the following examples. "A Midnight Clear" and "Blast Furnace" demonstrate his talent that has been putting mental and spiritual capacities to the stretch since his death in 1980.

I share them with you because with the passage of time I no longer turn away from the memories they stir within me. They bring strength to my soul. I pray that you'll find similar strength as his words become part of you.

A MIDNIGHT CLEAR

Outside the while-u-wait key shop at Sears
They tinkle a raucous salvation.
Three magi with brass and one tuba
Turn blue, but play on, but plead on,
Untuning the silent night
With God-rest-ye-merriment.
Above the lowing of key grinder they play,
Through barn blasts of popcorn air,
To sore and frayed masses
Of shepherdless Herods and sheepilates
In mail-order spirit. Hands
Just homaged to Claus clutch Christ-childs
Dressed in the highest
Styles in acetate swaddling,
Bought for 23 pieces unearthed
From pockets now empty, now
Shrunken and barren.
Eyes downcast, they pass the magi
And travel rough roads
From manger to mountains
To private Golgothas, hills far away,

They pass over the bleak veil of snow
To cold, myrrhthless homes
Where tinseled trees wait
For the Christ-child.
There is need of a shepherd,
There is use for a lamb.

BLAST FURNACE

Create me a clean, O hearth-God!
Unearth and crack, hammer, crush me,
With blast furnace breath burn,
Unblemish, melt me.
And sear, smelt
But spare
Me.
I am
Too much in me,
Too much dirt,
Dross and clay.
These are mine
O earth-God,
Mine them!
Do not cast out but recast in
Thy kingdom-come-will-be-done
shape.